A TRAINER'S GUIDE TO

THE CREATIVE CURRICULUM®

FOR INFANTS, TODDLERS & TWOS

Kai-leé Berke

Diane Trister Dodge

Sherrie Rudick

Teaching Strategies Inc.
Washington, DC

Editor: Nancy Guadagno
Cover and book design: Carla Uriona
Cover illustration: Jennifer Barrett O'Connell
Layout and production: Jeff Cross and Abner Nieves

Teaching Strategies, Inc.
P.O. Box 42243
Washington, DC 20015
www.TeachingStrategies.com

ISBN: 978-1-933021-37-9

Teaching Strategies and *The Creative Curriculum* names and logos are
registered trademarks of Teaching Strategies, Inc., Washington, DC.

Library of Congress Cataloging-in-Publication Data

Berke, Kai-lee.
  A trainer's guide to the creative curriculum for infants, toddlers & twos /
by Kai-lee Berke, Diane Trister Dodge, and Sherrie Rudick.
     p. cm.
  Includes bibliographical references.
   ISBN 978-1-933021-37-9
1. Education, Preschool--Curricula--United States--Handbooks,
manuals, etc. 2. Child care--United States--Handbooks, manuals, etc. 3.
Curriculum planning--United States--Handbooks, manuals, etc. 4. Child
development--United States--Handbooks, manuals, etc. I. Dodge, Diane
Trister. II. Rudick, Sherrie. III. Title.
  LB1140.4.B456 2007
  372.19--dc22
                              2007023507

Printed and bound in the United States of America

2012   2011   2010   2009
6   5   4   3

Table of Contents

Handouts

For easy printing, each handout is included as a separate PDF document on the CD that accompanies this *Trainer's Guide*.

Part 1: Workshops on Introducing the Components

Part 2: Workshops on Routines

Part 3: Workshops on Experiences

Acknowledgments

When we began the process of writing this *Trainer's Guide*, we challenged ourselves to design a range of creative ways for trainers to present the content of each aspect of *The Creative Curriculum for Infants, Toddlers & Twos*, and to convey the importance of building relationships as a central theme in caring for children under age 3. Some teachers may read *The Creative Curriculum* on their own and use it to guide their everyday practices. However, we recognize that most teachers learn most easily about the value of using a comprehensive curriculum linked to ongoing assessment when they attend training seminars or courses that engage them in collaborative learning and encourage them to share their experiences. Members of our Professional Development Trainer Network (PDN) provide this type of professional development experience every day in their work with teachers. We therefore invited them to help us begin the process of designing content-rich, engaging training sessions.

Our first step was to bring together several staff development specialists for a Training Summit. We spent 2 days brainstorming ideas for introducing the components of *The Creative Curriculum*, the routines, and each of the experiences. We thank Donna Bloomer, Gail Kelso, Jean Monroe, Sarah Semlak, and Diane Woodard for participating in this process with us. They generously shared their ideas, reviewed drafts of each section, and provided invaluable feedback. To pilot the workshops, we also turned to trainers in our PDN. We particularly want to thank Sarah Semlak and Vilma Williams for sharing their experiences and helping us to improve the workshop activities. We are indebted to Sue Mistrett, Product Development Associate at Teaching Strategies, who helped us address the topic of inclusion. Her thoughtful suggestions and a new activity were incorporated into the final draft. We also thank Bonnie Kittredge for sharing an idea that became one of our workshops.

When the writing process was complete, we gave the document to our very capable editorial staff. We thank Nancy Guadagno, who challenged us to rewrite anything that was unclear, ensured consistency in the format of each section, and edited every page of this book. We thank Laurie Taub and our able copy editors Rachel Friedlander Tickner and Vijay Simhan as well. The beautiful format and design of the book makes the content easily accessible to users. We thank Carla Uriona, Creative Services Director, for the design of the book and Jeff Cross and Abner Nieves, Creative Services Specialists, for their meticulous work on layout.

We hope that this *Trainer's Guide* will give staff development specialists, program directors, college instructors, and all users a wealth of ideas for introducing teachers to the rich content in *The Creative Curriculum for Infants, Toddlers & Twos*. It is our hope that the strategies we offer will inspire and enable teachers to internalize and effectively implement *The Creative Curriculum* in their everyday work with children and families.

Introduction

The Creative Curriculum® for Infants, Toddlers & Twos (hereafter referred to as *The Creative Curriculum*) is a comprehensive curriculum that provides explicit guidance on establishing and sustaining a high-quality program for the care and education of very young children. It describes the theory and research that are the foundation of *The Creative Curriculum*, and it applies this knowledge to everyday practices, giving teachers a road map for caring and teaching. Some teachers will pick up *The Creative Curriculum*, read it, and use it independently. Other teachers will need someone to guide them through the content and help them to apply the practices in their classrooms.

The purpose of this Trainer's Guide is to support the critically important role of program administrators, education coordinators, and staff development specialists who are responsible for helping teachers learn about and implement *The Creative Curriculum*. It can also be used by teacher educators who wish to incorporate the workshop activities into courses and seminars. You are the people who bring *The Creative Curriculum* to life.

How This *Trainer's Guide* Is Organized

The first section of *A Trainer's Guide* helps you develop a plan for implementing *The Creative Curriculum* in your program. The remainder of the book presents the workshops. Each workshop series begins with a description of the purpose of the workshops and the important ideas to be learned. Part I contains workshops that explore the foundation and the five components of *The Creative Curriculum*. Part II contains the workshops on the five routines, and Part III contains the workshops on the eight experiences that are presented in *The Creative Curriculum*. All of these workshops address how to support children's development and learning, how to create an environment for the routine or experience, and how to care for and teach children throughout the day.

A chart at the beginning of every workshop series identifies the major points to be covered in each workshop, the materials and supplies (including handouts) that are needed, the pages from *The Creative Curriculum* that are referenced during the activity, and the approximate amount of time required. Because the purpose of *A Trainer's Guide* is to help staff development professionals work with teachers to learn *The Creative Curriculum*, the content of the workshops mirrors the content presented in each chapter of *The Creative Curriculum*.

The workshop instructions have five parts. A list of the **Materials** needed for the workshop is given in the left-hand column, including a small image of each handout to be used. The CD in the back of the book contains files for all handouts in a format suitable for printing. The **Preparation** section explains what to do to get ready to lead the workshop. The **Introduction** gives talking points for beginning the workshop. The **Activity** section guides the trainer in conducting that workshop's learning activity or activities. Each workshop ends with **Summary** points to be made.

Planning for Training

Most workshops are designed for 30- to 90-minute periods. Times will vary depending on group size and participants' knowledge, experience, interests, and level of engagement. This design allows programs that have only short periods available for training to offer engaging activities that can be built upon over time. For programs wanting lengthier, more intensive training, a variety of workshops are offered from which to choose.

The activities suggested in *A Trainer's Guide* engage attendees in many ways and at many different levels. Unless indicated otherwise, the activities in each workshop assume that participants are able to work at tables in groups of 4–8 people. In some activities, participants will work alone, in other activities they will work with a partner, and in other activities they will work with the whole group. Many activities call for sharing information, brainstorming ideas, or practicing new strategies to use with children. Having small groups seated at tables encourages discussion and collaboration.

Here are some suggestions to consider as you use *A Trainer's Guide*:

- Thoroughly read *The Creative Curriculum*. As the workshop presenter, you will have more credibility if you have a thorough knowledge of the book and are able to answer participants' specific questions about its content.

- Be selective about the workshops you want to present. You will find a wide variety of workshops on many topics. Select workshops based on what you know about your group, the time available, and what you are comfortable presenting.

- Know your participants. For example, if you have a group that only works with young infants, you may choose not to do workshops that are geared to older toddlers and 2-year-olds, such as the one on toilet learning.

- Prepare ahead of time. For some activities, we have listed possible responses to questions and brainstorming. Where we have not done that, write down the responses you expect to hear and prepare your own stories to share. Sharing personal stories is a powerful way to make people comfortable and more willing to share their own experiences.

- Adapt the activities and instructions to fit your situation. For example, if time is limited, you might decide to have each group respond to one question on a handout rather than have all of the groups do all the tasks. If you do this, allow time for the groups to share their ideas.

- Use your own words. Wherever you see text presented in bullet format, these are suggested words, points, and questions. Use these suggestions as talking points and put them into your own words.

- Read aloud if necessary. If some of the participants in your groups are not fast readers, consider reading aloud the scenarios in some of the workshops or asking participants to read the related sections of *The Creative Curriculum* prior to coming to the training.

- Ensure that each participant has a copy of *The Creative Curriculum*. Because the underlying goal of the workshops is to familiarize participants with the content of *The Creative Curriculum* and apply it in their own settings, it is best if all participants have their own books. Provide small sticky notes during training and encourage participants to use them to mark pages and write notes.

Implementing *The Creative Curriculum* in Your Program

A curriculum is like a road map: It helps you get where you want to go. Curriculum implementation means taking that map and beginning the journey. Before starting, you will need to think about who will be traveling with you and how you will support each other along the way. While the map will show you where you are going, you will have to make choices about what routes to take. As you make stops along your journey, you may choose to stay longer in some places than others. New people may join you as you travel, offering innovative ideas and fresh perspectives. Knowing that there will be bumps in the road and detours along the way, you must plan ahead of time for how you will move smoothly through these challenges, using your road map and your support team as your guide.

As you begin to develop a plan for helping teachers learn about and implement *The Creative Curriculum*, it will be helpful to think about the different phases of your implementation journey. Each of these phases is described below.

Create a Shared Vision for Implementation

A first step in preparing to implement *The Creative Curriculum* is to build a shared vision with your teachers and other staff members. You will be able to begin and maintain curriculum implementation when you have this clearly written statement. A vision helps to identify direction and purpose for the staff.

In creating a shared vision, think about how you would like curriculum implementation to look in the future. Imagine it is 5 years from now and you and your staff have done an excellent job of implementing *The Creative Curriculum* in your program. Consider the following questions:

- What are the teachers and other staff members doing? How do they feel about *The Creative Curriculum* and their work with children and families?

- What are the children doing? Do they seem comfortable and happy when they arrive each day?

- What are the families thinking and feeling about *The Creative Curriculum* and about your program?

- What do the rooms look like?

- What are people saying about your program?

- What requirements is your program successfully meeting (e.g., Head Start Program Performance Standards, voluntary accreditation standards, state requirements, mandated outcomes) by implementing *The Creative Curriculum*?

Once the vision is defined, your staff can use it to guide their implementation of *The Creative Curriculum*. With every step you take, revisit your vision to ensure that you are moving toward your intended goal: excellence in implementation.

Determine Training Needs

The next step is to determine the training needs of the staff members who will implement *The Creative Curriculum*. Many variables have an impact on where you decide to start, including:

- Staff members' backgrounds, interests, and experiences

- Staff members' familiarity with *The Creative Curriculum* and *The Creative Curriculum* system

- The degree to which each room reflects *The Creative Curriculum* environment guidelines and the staff are already carrying out pieces of the system

- The outside challenges, priorities, and requirements that your program faces

- The opportunities, time, and resources that can be allocated for staff development

To help ensure that teachers receive the training and support they need, every program should develop an annual training plan specifying the variety of professional development opportunities that will be offered and when. For assistance in determining training needs, use *The Implementation & Planning Tool for The Creative Curriculum for Infants, Toddlers & Twos*. This publication is a tool for establishing the degree to which each aspect of *The Creative Curriculum* is being implemented as intended. It can be used to assess staff development and other program needs.

Use *The Implementation & Planning Tool*

The Implementation & Planning Tool identifies the key aspects of *The Creative Curriculum* in a checklist format. It is designed to involve teachers in identifying aspects of *The Creative Curriculum* they are already implementing successfully and aspects for which they need more information, skills, materials, and instruction. The data gathered with this tool can help you select areas on which to focus your training and support.

Teachers can begin by reading through *The Implementation & Planning Tool* and marking the items that are already in place. When they first begin to use it, most teachers are reassured when they discover that many of their current practices are a part of *The Creative Curriculum*. Teachers are not as overwhelmed when they can see, in writing, that they already are implementing various aspects of *The Creative Curriculum*. They also identify specific areas where they need to learn more, practices they need to incorporate, and materials they need to acquire in order to implement *The Creative Curriculum* fully.

Trainers can review the teachers' self-assessments to see how to focus the training. A trainer may have the opportunity to visit the rooms and complete *The Implementation & Planning Tool* before designing a training plan for a program. The trainer can meet with the program administrator to discuss the findings and focus training on the specific aspects of *The Creative Curriculum* that need the most attention. The amount of time spent on various topics can be adjusted according to these findings.

Administrators can use *The Implementation & Planning Tool* as a tool to help keep the program on track and to assess the degree of implementation in each room. After teachers have learned about new parts of *The Creative Curriculum*, administrators can use *The Implementation & Planning Tool* to follow up with the teachers in their rooms to see if what was learned is being applied. Administrators can also use *The Implementation & Planning Tool* to see what materials, furnishings, and equipment should be purchased to help teachers effectively implement *The Creative Curriculum*. These room visits and their follow-up analysis will help administrators develop a training plan for their program.

Develop a Training Plan

In developing your training plan, keep in mind what is known about how adults learn best.

Adults bring a great deal of experience and knowledge to their work and to the learning process. Training is more meaningful if it builds on the life experiences of each person. Use approaches that encourage teachers to think about their own experiences and use the insights they have gained in their work with children and families. Meaningful learning occurs when people can make connections between what they know and what they are learning.

Adults need time to assimilate new ideas and information. Workshops spaced over time are more effective than intensive training crammed into a few days. People need time to think about what they learned, try out new ideas, and come back to talk about their experiences and what they observed.

Adults are often uneasy about taking risks. Keep in mind that when you ask people to try something new, they may feel uncomfortable. It is safer and more comfortable to keep doing things the same old way. People are more willing to change, however, if they see a reason to try a new approach and if they know that experimentation is welcomed rather than discouraged. Make it safe for people to take risks by reassuring them that mistakes are part of the learning process and we all can learn from them.

Think about how you will plan for orientation, classroom support, ongoing training and support, staff time, and workshops.

Orientation: How many days can I allocate to introduce *The Creative Curriculum*? Who should attend? Where will the training take place? How will I orient staff members hired mid-year?

Classroom support: How often will I observe in the teacher's rooms? When will I make these observations? How will I build in time for follow-up conversations and feedback?

Ongoing training and support: What arrangements can I make for teachers to meet together to share ideas and experiences in implementing *The Creative Curriculum*? What other programs might teachers visit? How can I continue to guide teachers in using *The Creative Curriculum*?

Staff time: How will I provide time for teachers to participate in training sessions? Do I have money in my budget to compensate them for their time so that we can hold training outside of the workday? How often will the staff need to meet together to plan?

Workshops: What workshops will deepen teachers' understanding of *The Creative Curriculum*? How can I space workshops to allow teachers time to implement the ideas they learn?

As you plan for staff development, try to have all training experiences count toward meeting the teachers' professional development requirements. For most state, federal, and national regulatory agencies, this involves verifying that formal training sessions—such as courses, workshops, study groups, and seminars—are led by certified trainers; documenting the hours of attendance and completion of assignments; and showing that these experiences were in one of the core competencies outlined by the early childhood profession. Whenever possible, college credit should be offered. Training experiences and course credits should lead to increased professional responsibilities and compensation.

Introduce *The Creative Curriculum*

It is very important that everyone implementing *The Creative Curriculum* has a common understanding of its philosophy and the system and knows how to apply these concepts and resources to everyday decision making. If you are introducing *The Creative Curriculum*, plan for at least 4 full days of training and arrange for all staff members to attend. If you have been using *The Creative Curriculum* and your staff members are familiar with the system, you still might find it useful to provide an overview of the components before you focus intensively on specific topics. The "Setting the Stage" workshops in this trainer's guide offer guidance on how to do this.

Deliver the introductory training with enthusiasm, linking the content of the workshops to the shared vision that you created with your staff for curriculum implementation. You may find it helpful to contact the professional development department at Teaching Strategies, Inc., to schedule an on-site training with a professional from our Staff Development Network.

To help teachers get started, allow time to work with them in their rooms on setting up and equipping areas for the routines and experiences, labeling materials, and preparing for the first few days of putting the curriculum into practice. Refer them to the sections in *The Creative Curriculum* that address these topics.

One of the strengths of *The Creative Curriculum* is the link between its goals and objectives for children and its Developmental Continuum Assessment System. Although assessment is an integral part of implementing *The Creative Curriculum*, you will have to judge the best time to introduce this system to the staff. It is most important to focus first on getting started with *The Creative Curriculum*. Once teachers have established a responsive environment, created systems for routines and experiences, and developed trusting relationships with the children in their care, you can plan to introduce assessment.

Provide Ongoing Training and Support

The most important phase in implementing any curriculum is the ongoing support and training teachers receive through the year. This is when you can individualize your training and support based on your observations and the results of a teacher's self-assessment. Together, you can design a staff development plan that reflects each teacher's preferred way of learning and the topics of greatest importance to the teacher. Here are some options for offering ongoing training and support.

Observation and support. There is no substitute for observing and supporting teachers in their rooms. Only by visiting rooms can you determine exactly how well teachers understand and to what extent they are implementing *The Creative Curriculum*. You will also learn about particular challenges each teacher has encountered and how you can offer support.

Workshops, seminars, and courses. The orientation is just the beginning of training on *The Creative Curriculum*. Arrange for ongoing training through workshops, seminars, and courses that address different topics in depth. Select workshop activities that will work for your group of teachers and that correspond to their interests and the aspects of curriculum implementation that need strengthening. Training is best provided in an ongoing series, not one isolated event, so staff members are able to make connections with the content and build their knowledge from one workshop to the next.

Weekly e-mails or mini-newsletters. Once a week, send a short e-mail or distribute a mini-newsletter to the staff highlighting a section of *The Creative Curriculum* that is relevant to what is occurring in your program. These short notes can include quotes from the book and refer the staff to the pages that will help them address an issue, such as "Holding Conferences With Families" (pages 198–200) and "Supporting Children and Families During Hellos and Good-Byes" (pages 225–226).

Staff meetings. Most programs have regular staff meetings. Try to use some of this time for discussing one aspect of *The Creative Curriculum*. You might have everyone read a section that is particularly relevant to the staff and come prepared to discuss their reactions, thoughts, and questions. You might choose one of the workshops from this book that addresses a topic that will benefit your whole staff. Having an agenda item for each meeting that is related to *The Creative Curriculum* reminds everyone that the book is a guide they can consult regularly, not something to gather dust on a shelf.

Visiting other rooms and programs. Teachers can learn a great deal by observing other rooms where *The Creative Curriculum* is being implemented well. Such visits might reveal the effect of good room arrangement, positive adult-child interactions, successful systems for managing routines, and smooth transitions. Participating in the visit enables you to focus the teachers' observations and discuss what you and the teachers observe.

Mentoring. The first year of working with infants, toddlers, and twos in a group setting can be overwhelming. An experienced staff member can help a new teacher with the daily details of working in the program, as well as offer practical tips on how to implement *The Creative Curriculum*. A mentoring relationship can be a growth experience for both the mentor and the new staff member.

Connecting via the Internet. Today, teachers can learn from their colleagues in their schools or centers and, through technology, by networking with teachers all over the world. The Internet provides teachers with access to a variety of resources concerning early childhood education. The Teaching Strategies Web site, www.TeachingStrategies.com, features an e-mail discussion group on *The Creative Curriculum*. Participants submit questions on their use of *The Creative Curriculum*. Answers are provided by other users from around the world—and sometimes by Teaching Strategies staff members and authors. This is a wonderful forum for sharing experiences and ideas.

Review Progress and Plan for the Future

Periodically during the year, go back to the data you have collected and check on your program, staff, and children's progress. Reviewing child outcome data will provide you with information on how program changes through implementation have influenced children's progress. Repeating sections of *The Implementation & Planning Tool* that were low-scoring areas for each staff member will let you know what progress individual teachers have made. As you review your data, consider the following questions:

- What parts of the program are currently meeting the shared vision for implementation?

- In what areas have teachers and children made the most progress? What actions and program improvements can you attribute to that progress?

- What areas still need more attention?

- What goals did you meet throughout the year?

- What areas do teachers still need to explore?

- How can we continue to move closer to our goal of excellence in implementation?

After reflecting on the data, you can work with staff to revise staff development plans.

Setting the Stage

Workshops

⚙ WORKSHOP	🔑 KEY POINTS	📋 MATERIALS	⏱ TIME (minutes)
Overview of *The Creative Curriculum® for Infants, Toddlers & Twos* (p. 2)	*The Creative Curriculum* explains all aspects of a developmentally appropriate program and leads you through the process of planning and implementing every aspect of caring for and teaching infants, toddlers, and twos.	☐ Sticky notes, flags, or divider tabs ☐ Handout SET–1. The Organization of *The Creative Curriculum® for Infants, Toddlers & Twos* ☐ Handout SET–2. A Scavenger Hunt: *The Creative Curriculum® for Infants, Toddlers & Twos,* 2nd Edition ☐ *The Creative Curriculum*	60
Where Are We Going? How Do We Get There? (p. 8)	The fundamental beliefs that underlie *The Creative Curriculum* emphasize the importance of the relationships you build with children and with families, and how you help children develop critically important social and emotional skills.	☐ Chart paper ☐ Markers ☐ Handout SET–3. Where Are We Going? How Do We Get There? ☐ The *Creative Curriculum,* pp. xiii–xiv	45
Wall of Fame (p. 12)	Knowing the research and theory behind *The Creative Curriculum* enables you to explain not only *what* you do in your work with young children but also *why.*	☐ Chart paper ☐ Markers ☐ Assorted art supplies ☐ Handout SET–4. Theory and Research Behind *The Creative Curriculum® for Infants, Toddlers & Twos* ☐ The *Creative Curriculum,* pp. 2–17	60

Overview of *The Creative Curriculum® for Infants, Toddlers & Twos*

☐ Sticky notes, flags, or divider tabs

☐ Handout SET–1

☐ Handout SET–2

☐ *The Creative Curriculum*

Preparation

Copy handout SET–1, "The Organization of *The Creative Curriculum® for Infants, Toddlers & Twos,*" and handout SET–2, "A Scavenger Hunt: *The Creative Curriculum® for Infants, Toddlers & Twos,* 2nd Edition."

Read the "Introduction," pages xiii–xviii, to *The Creative Curriculum.*

Place sticky notes, flags, or divider tabs on each table.

Introduction

Make the following points:

- The care that infants, toddlers, and twos receive and their experiences during their first 3 years of life strongly influence how they view the world, how they relate to others, and their ability to succeed as learners.

- As a teacher, you have a unique opportunity to make a difference in the lives of very young children and their families.

Activity

Go through the following discussion encouraging the participants to turn to the relevant section in the book as you describe *The Creative Curriculum.*

What Is Curriculum?

- A curriculum is a like a road map; it helps you get where you want to go.

- A comprehensive curriculum like *The Creative Curriculum* includes goals and objectives for children's learning in all areas of development: social/emotional, physical, cognitive, and language.

- Goals and objectives show you where you want to go.

- The curriculum tells you how to get there.

- Curriculum is the what, why, how, and when of providing a high-quality program.

Highlights of the Second Edition

This new edition retains its focus on building relationships, responsive care, and routines and experiences. It updates the first edition in many important ways:

- Uses the same organizational structure as *The Creative Curriculum for Preschool* to provide continuity for programs

- Introduces *The Creative Curriculum Developmental Continuum for Infants, Toddlers & Twos* to help teachers thoughtfully observe children and use what they learn to be responsive to children's interests and needs

- Addresses language and literacy, math, and science, because very young children are already exploring ideas and developing important skills that become the building blocks for future learning

- Offers specific guidance on how to meet the needs of 2-year-olds, dual-language learners, and children with disabilities

- Highlights the research and theory on which *The Creative Curriculum* is based and the implications for everyday practices

Trainer's Note: If you are working with a group that is new to *The Creative Curriculum*, you can discuss these points as being among its highlights. If you are working with a program that has been using the first edition of *The Creative Curriculum*, emphasize that these are differences between the first and second editions.

How the Curriculum Is Organized

- *The Creative Curriculum* rests on a solid foundation of theory and research.

- Its organizational structure has five components that help you make good decisions about the routines and experiences you provide for infants, toddlers, and twos.

- The curriculum components, shown on handout SET–1, form an organizational structure for decision making. They are discussed in Part 1, "Components of the Curriculum," the first five chapters of the book.

Have participants turn to page xvii in the "Introduction" and make the following points:

- *The Creative Curriculum* describes how you plan and how you provide responsive care for children in four age groups.

- The ages overlap a bit because children develop on individual timetables and because programs define age groups in a number of ways.

- Every chapter provides examples of what children do at different ages and what responsive care is like.

As you discuss the following, have participants turn to each corresponding section and use the sticky notes, flags, or divider tabs to mark the first page of each chapter in their copy of *The Creative Curriculum*.

Foundation: Theory and Research

- This preliminary chapter, "The Foundation," summarizes the major theories and research that underlie the focus of *The Creative Curriculum* on the importance of meeting basic needs, fostering social/emotional development, developing secure attachments, and supporting cognition and brain development.

- This chapter also explains how *The Creative Curriculum* helps you put those theories and research into practice.

Knowing Infants, Toddlers, and Twos

- "Knowing Infants, Toddlers, and Twos" is the first component, and chapter 1, of *The Creative Curriculum.* It describes the social/emotional, physical, cognitive, and language development of young infants, mobile infants, toddlers, and 2-year-olds.

- It discusses the characteristics and experiences that make children unique, including temperament, life experiences, dual-language learning, and disabilities.

- It presents the curriculum goals and objectives for children and the *Developmental Continuum*, a tool for observing children's development and following their progress in relation to 21 objectives.

- The four areas of development and their corresponding goals on the *Developmental Continuum* are:

    - Social/Emotional development—Goal 1: To learn about self and others

    - Physical development—Goal 2: To learn about moving

    - Cognitive development—Goal 3: To learn about the world

    - Language development—Goal 4: To learn about communicating

- While it is helpful to consider these areas for planning and discussion, development does not actually divide into neat categories. Rather, the four categories are closely related and often overlap.

Creating a Responsive Environment

- The second component of *The Creative Curriculum* is "Creating a Responsive Environment." This chapter offers guidance and specific strategies for setting up the physical environment for routines and experiences in ways that address the developing abilities and interests of infants, toddlers, and twos.

- It shows you how to create a daily schedule and weekly plans that provide direction while allowing you to be responsive to what you learn about each child.

What Children Are Learning

- "What Children Are Learning," the third component of the curriculum, shows how the responsive relationship you form with each child, the interactions you have every day, and the materials and experiences you offer become the building blocks for successful learning.

- Language and literacy, mathematical relationships, and scientific explorations are all addressed in this chapter.

Caring and Teaching

- The fourth component, "Caring and Teaching," describes the varied and interrelated roles of teachers who work with infants, toddlers, and twos.

- It offers strategies for building positive relationships with each child and helping children develop self-regulation.

- It shows how to guide children's learning during daily routines and everyday experiences.

- "Caring and Teaching" also explains the role of ongoing observation and assessment in learning about each child, following children's progress, and planning.

Building Partnerships With Families

- The fifth and last component, "Building Partnerships With Families," explores the benefits of working with families as partners in the care of their children.

- It explains how partnerships are built by exchanging information daily, welcoming families and involving them in all aspects of the program, communicating in respectful ways, and working through differences in ways that sustain the partnership and benefit each child.

Routines and Experiences

- Part 2 of *The Creative Curriculum* describes five routines. Each of these five chapters explains how a daily routine is an important part of the curriculum and an important time to put research and theory into practice.

- The chapters explain how routines are opportunities to build relationships with children that promote the development of trust and autonomy. The one-on-one time you spend easing a child and family through hellos and good-byes, diapering and toileting, feeding, dressing, and soothing a child to sleep helps infants, toddlers, and twos learn to trust and feel secure with you. As they gain new skills and can participate more actively in routines, children develop a sense of their competence.

- Part 3 of the *The Creative Curriculum* presents eight different experiences you can offer young children.

- It discusses how to select materials for different ages and ways to engage children in playing with toys, imitating and pretending, enjoying stories and books, connecting with music and movement, creating with art, tasting and preparing food, exploring sand and water, and going outdoors.

These chapters also explain that, while planning for these experiences is important, you are really planning only for possibilities and you must always be open to following children's interests and addressing their needs.

Activity

Distribute handout SET–2, "A Scavenger Hunt: *The Creative Curriculum*® *for Infants, Toddlers & Twos*, 2nd Edition." Invite participants to work individually, in pairs, or in small groups to find answers in *The Creative Curriculum* to the questions on the handout.

Summary

Make the following points:

- *The Creative Curriculum* explains all aspects of a developmentally appropriate program.

- It leads you through the process of planning and implementing every aspect of caring for and teaching infants, toddlers, and 2-year-olds.

Where Are We Going? How Do We Get There?

☐ Chart paper
☐ Markers
☐ Handout SET–3
☐ *The Creative Curriculum*, pp. xiii to xiv

Preparation

Review the "Introduction," pages xiii–xviii, to *The Creative Curriculum*.

Make copies of handout SET–3, "Where Are We Going? How Do We Get There?"

Introduction

Make the following points:

- The introduction to *The Creative Curriculum* states, "A curriculum is like a road map; it helps you get where you want to go" (page xiii).

- Therefore, it is important to be clear about where we are going and the best route to take to get there.

Activity

Give the following instructions:

- It's 20 years from today and you are having a reunion with the children who currently are in your program. They are all grown up.

- What kind of people would you like them to become? What characteristics and abilities might they have that will make you feel that you helped to lay the foundation for their success?

- Take some time to think about this and then, in the first box on handout SET–3, "Where Are We Going? How Do We Get There?" write down words or phrases to describe what you hope to see.

Allow 5 minutes for individual work. Then have participants share their ideas with the others at their table.

When you feel the group at each table has had sufficient time to discuss their ideas, ask each group to share one characteristic. Record their ideas on chart paper and continue having each group report until all their ideas are listed.

Possible responses:

Confident

Happy

Loving

Independent

Goal oriented

Physically and emotionally healthy

Able to make friends

Good problem solvers

Able to communicate thoughts and feelings in words

Good readers

Able to establish boundaries in relationships

Humorous

Enthusiastic learners

Respectful of others and of the environment

Motivated

Willing to try new things

Happy to be who they are

Comment on the ideas that have been shared, pointing out how many are social and emotional skills. Then give the following instructions:

- If these are the characteristics we feel are most important—where we are going—then let's think about how we will get there.

- Take a few minutes to think about what you need to do every day to nurture these characteristics. What are the most important aspects of your work?

- Record your ideas in the second box on your handout.

After allowing sufficient time for each person to record a few ideas, invite them to share with others at their table. Then have each group report one idea at a time and record the ideas on chart paper.

Refer participants to the "Introduction," pages xiii to xiv, to *The Creative Curriculum*, which describes the curriculum as a road map for getting where you want to go. Compare their list to the "Fundamental Beliefs" that underlie *The Creative Curriculum*.

Summary

Make the following points:

- The fundamental beliefs that underlie *The Creative Curriculum* emphasize the importance of the relationships you build with children and families and how you help children develop critically important social and emotional skills.

- These beliefs, and the approaches to caring for and teaching infants, toddlers, and twos described in *The Creative Curriculum,* are the best route to achieving your long-term goals for the children you teach today.

Notes:

Wall of Fame

☐ Chart Paper
☐ Markers
☐ Assorted art supplies
☐ Handout SET–4
☐ *The Creative Curriculum*, pp. 2–17

Preparation

Copy handout SET–4, "Theory and Research Behind *The Creative Curriculum®️ for Infants, Toddlers & Twos.*"

Review the charts on pages 4, 7, 11, and 17 in *The Creative Curriculum.*

Introduction

Make the following points:

- *The Creative Curriculum* is based on accepted theories and research that explain how children develop and learn.

- When you understand the theory and research, you will know what you are doing and why and will be able to make informed decisions about daily classroom practice and your work with individual children.

- The purpose of this workshop is to introduce the theory and research that form the foundation of *The Creative Curriculum* and to consider how each affects program design, daily practice, and decision making. Additional research and reports are referenced at the end of the book.

Activity

Explain that in this activity participants will build a Wall of Fame to represent the findings of important theorists and researchers in the field of early childhood education.

Have participants form eight groups. Assign each group one of the following theorists or research topics:

- Meeting Basic Needs (Maslow, Brazelton, and Greenspan)
- Erik Erikson
- Stanley Greenspan
- Attachment
- Resilience
- Jean Piaget
- Lev Vygotsky
- Learning and the Brain

Give the following instructions:

- Pages 2–17 in your book explain the theory and research that are the foundation of *The Creative Curriculum*. Find and read the sections describing the theorist or research you have been assigned. Then talk among yourselves to share what you have learned.

- Next, use the art material on your table to make a poster that highlights the main ideas.

- Turn to handout SET–4, "Theory and Research Behind *The Creative Curriculum® for Infants, Toddlers & Twos*." Review the findings of this theory or research and discuss the implications for classroom practice. Consider how these ideas influence what you do every day; record your thoughts in column 3 of the handout.

- When finished, you will present your posters highlighting the findings and share the implications for practice.

Allow time for the groups to complete their posters and present them. During the presentations, have other participants record their practices in the last column of the handout. Add any comments you think are needed.

After each presentation, hang the poster on the wall to create the Wall of Fame. Display them throughout the training and revisit them as the other parts of *The Creative Curriculum* are discussed.

Summary

- These theories and this research influenced the design of *The Creative Curriculum,* the ideas about children, and the recommendations that the authors make to teachers.

- Understanding theory and research about how infants, toddlers, and twos develop and learn helps you plan a program and work with children in ways that build trusting relationships and match the ways that children learn.

- Knowing the research and theory behind *The Creative Curriculum* enables you to explain not only *what* you do in your work with young children but also *why*.

Knowing Infants, Toddlers, and Twos

Purpose

In order to plan and implement an appropriate and responsive program for infants, toddlers, and twos, teachers must know what young children are like developmentally as well as what makes each child unique. This means understanding the sequence of growth in social/emotional, physical, cognitive, and language development. It also means learning about each child's strengths, interests and experiences; challenges each child likes or is frustrated by; and ways each child is comforted. By knowing children, teachers can respond in ways that address each child's needs and can build trusting relationships with the children in their care.

This workshop series addresses basic knowledge of child development and individual differences, and introduces the *The Creative Curriculum® Developmental Continuum for Infants, Toddlers & Twos*. Participants learn how to apply this knowledge to their everyday teaching practices.

Big Ideas

- Child development is the accepted body of knowledge about how children grow and learn in four areas: social/emotional, physical, cognitive, and language development.

- These developmental areas are closely related: Development in one area affects and is influenced by development in all other areas.

- Understanding the stages of development for young infants, mobile infants, toddlers, and twos enables teachers to plan appropriate experiences for children.

- To provide individualized care and learning experiences, teachers need to consider the individual characteristics and experiences that affect how each child responds to adults, relates to other children, and learns.

- The goals and objectives of *The Creative Curriculum* address important aspects of a child's development and learning that can be influenced by a teacher's care and teaching.

Knowing Infants, Toddlers, and Twos

Workshops

⚙ WORKSHOP	🔑 KEY POINTS	📄 MATERIALS	⏱ TIME (minutes)
Portraits of Child Development: What Infants, Toddlers, and Twos Are Like (p. 18)	Knowing how infants, toddlers, and twos develop is the starting point for every teacher using *The Creative Curriculum*. Knowing infants, toddlers, and twos means not only appreciating general patterns of growth of all children but also appreciating the many ways in which each child is unique.	☐ Chart paper ☐ Markers ☐ *The Creative Curriculum*, pp. 22–34	60
Understanding That Each Child Is Unique: Life Circumstances (p. 22)	Being aware of children's individual life circumstances helps you understand the events that may affect their development and learning.	☐ Handout 1A. Life Circumstances Thought Sheet ☐ *The Creative Curriculum*, p. 38	30
Understanding That Each Child Is Unique: Temperament (p. 24)	Knowing the temperaments of the children in your care can help you better understand how to support their development and learning.	☐ Handout 1B. Descriptions of Children ☐ Handout 1C. Comparing Characteristics of Temperament ☐ *The Creative Curriculum*, pp. 35–37	60
Understanding That Each Child Is Unique: Dual Language (p. 28)	A number of misconceptions about learning two languages can cause unnecessary anxiety for teachers and parents.	☐ Chart paper ☐ Markers	30

⬡ WORKSHOP	⚷ KEY POINTS	▤ MATERIALS	⏱ TIME (minutes)
Understanding That Each Child Is Unique: Disabilities (p. 32)	All children need to feel included and successful. *The Creative Curriculum* offers many strategies for supporting children with disabilities and their families.	☐ Handout 1D. Strategies for Supporting Children With Disabilities ☐ *The Creative Curriculum*	45
The Goals and Objectives of *The Creative Curriculum®* *for Infants, Toddlers & Twos* (p. 34)	To provide quality care, you need to know how children develop and what you want them to learn. The goals and objectives of *The Creative Curriculum* address the important aspects of a child's development and learning that can be influenced by your care and teaching.	☐ *The Creative Curriculum*, p. 44 and Appendix, p. 424, "Goals and Objectives at a Glance"	30
Looking at Development on a Continuum (p. 36)	The *Developmental Continuum* links directly to the goals and objectives of *The Creative Curriculum* and lays out the progression of development for each objective under its respective learning goal.	☐ Card stock ☐ Handout 1E. Continuum Cards for the Adult Objective "Uses a Cell Phone" ☐ Handout 1F. Continuum Cards for Goals and Objectives for Infants, Toddlers, and Twos ☐ *The Creative Curriculum*, pp. 45, 47–57	60

WORKSHOP

Portraits of Child Development:
What Infants, Toddlers, and Twos Are Like

☐ Chart paper
☐ Markers
☐ *The Creative Curriculum*, pp. 22–34

Preparation

Review pages 22–34 in *The Creative Curriculum.*

Introduction

Make the following points:

- Curriculum begins with knowing children.

- The first component of *The Creative Curriculum*, presented in chapter 1, "Knowing Infants, Toddlers, and Twos," describes the four areas of development: social/emotional, physical, cognitive, and language. Development in one area affects and is influenced by development in all other areas. Chapter 1 also discusses the characteristics and experiences that make each child unique.

- Young children's social/emotional development involves the way they feel about themselves, their understanding of feelings, their ability to regulate emotions and express them appropriately, and their capacity for building trusting relationships with others. Social/emotional development flourishes when children have close, supportive, and trusting relationships with adults.

- Physical development refers to gradually gaining control over large and small muscles. Gross motor skills allow a child to do such things as roll over, sit, crawl, walk, run, and throw a ball. Young children use fine motor skills, such as holding, pinching, and flexing fingers, when they hold a rattle, pick up a large bead with their thumb and forefinger, or scribble.

- Cognitive development involves the way children think, develop understandings of the world, and use what they learn to reason and solve problems. Infants, toddlers, and 2-year-olds interact with others and actively use all of their senses and motor skills to construct their own understandings of the people and objects in their environment.

- Language development is a major accomplishment during the first 3 years of life. Children progress from communicating needs through facial expressions, gestures, body movements, and crying to communicating through verbal or sign language. They can acquire a vocabulary of thousands of words and learn the rules for using them by being with adults who communicate with them, encourage their efforts to communicate, and guide their exploration and learning.

Activity

Tell participants that in this activity they will review what they know about the development of young infants, mobile infants, toddlers, and twos.

Divide participants into four groups by letting them choose the age group they know best: young infants, mobile infants, toddlers, or twos.

Give each group a sheet of chart paper and some markers.

Have participants open up to pages 22–34 in *The Creative Curriculum*. Explain the content organization of the section, "What Infants, Toddlers, and Twos Are Like."

Tell participants that their job is to create a portrait of a child in their assigned age group using words, symbols, and pictures. Describe children at that age. What are they like? What do they do? How do they behave? What kinds of things do they like and dislike? How do they express themselves? How do they interact with others? How are they developing socially, emotionally, physically, and cognitively? How is their language developing?

Allow about 15 minutes for small-group work. After the groups have had a chance to create their portraits, have each group share their work with the whole group.

Ask: "Why do you think it is important to know about child development? How do you use this knowledge in your program?"

Discuss their responses.

Possible responses:

To organize the environment

To make decisions about materials and experiences

To focus observations

For weekly planning

To guide expectations of children's behavior and development

Explain that in addition to knowing about typical patterns of development, it is also important to know about individual differences. Ask participants what factors can influence an individual child's development. Record their ideas on chart paper and discuss their responses.

Possible responses:

Family life

Home culture

Siblings

Temperament

Medical issues

Special needs

Length of time in care and school settings

Explain that a child's home culture can greatly influence the child's development and how that child demonstrates new skills and understandings. Instruct participants to read the sections on how culture might affect development on pages 25–26, 28, 31, and 34 in *The Creative Curriculum*.

Lead a discussion about their responses to these sections. Ask participants to share other examples from their own experiences.

Summary

Make the following points:

- Knowing how infants, toddlers, and twos develop is the starting point for using *The Creative Curriculum*.

- Knowing infants, toddlers, and twos means appreciating both the general patterns of growth in all children and the many ways in which each child is unique.

- Culture influences the way that children develop as well as the way that children demonstrate what they know and can do.

Understanding That Each Child Is Unique: Life Circumstances

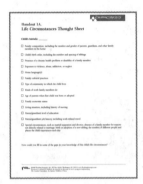

☐ Handout 1A
☐ *The Creative Curriculum,* p. 38

Preparation

Copy handout 1A, "Life Circumstances Thought Sheet."

Review pages 38–39 in *The Creative Curriculum.*

Introduction

Make the following points:

- Each child comes to you with different life circumstances.

- Life circumstances are one of the ways in which children are unique.

- Considering these circumstances will help you to understand how they affect the children you care for and teach.

Activity

Explain that in this activity, participants will have the opportunity to reflect on life circumstances that may affect children's development and learning.

Have participants open to page 38 in *The Creative Curriculum.* Review the bullet points related to life circumstances.

Distribute handout 1A, "Life Circumstances Thought Sheet."

Give the following instructions:

- Think of a child in your room and write his or her initials on the handout.

- Read each of the descriptions and put a check in the box if you know that information about the child you selected.

- When you are finished, find a partner and discuss what you were able to answer and what you could not.

- Together, brainstorm ways to find out what you may need to know.

After most participants are finished, have volunteers share their ideas.

Make the following points:

- Try to become knowledgeable about each child's circumstances when he or she enters your program.

- Talking with family members and taking notes about what you learn is an important first step.

- Encourage families to communicate with you about anything new taking place in their children's lives, and honor their style of communication.

- It takes time to develop trusting relationships with family members that encourage open communication. Remember to honor the confidentiality of information that family members share with you.

- If a family member shares information that you do not know how to handle, seek advice from your supervisor or an outside expert.

Summary

Make the following points:

- Knowing about children's individual life circumstances helps you understand events that may affect their development and learning.

- Developing trusting relationships with families and maintaining communication with them helps you stay informed about changes in a child's life.

Understanding That Each Child Is Unique: Temperament

☐ Handout 1B

☐ Handout 1C

☐ *The Creative Curriculum,* pp. 35–37

Preparation

Copy handout 1B, "Descriptions of Children," and cut apart the descriptions. Make enough so that each pair of participants can have one description.

Copy handout 1C, "Comparing Characteristics of Temperament."

Introduction

Make the following points:

- Children are born with behavioral styles called temperaments. For example, some children approach new situations cautiously, without a fuss, and adapt slowly. Others have an immediate positive response to new situations, are generally cheerful, and have regular patterns of behavior. Still others withdraw or cry in new situations.

- When you are aware of a child's temperament, you can sometimes predict how that child will behave in certain types of situations.

- Thinking about temperament may help you to understand and interpret children's behavior so you can act in ways that best meet children's needs.

Activity 1

Explain that in this activity, participants will review nine characteristics of temperament and consider related appropriate teaching practices.

Have participants turn to page 36 in *The Creative Curriculum*. Review the nine characteristics with them and then make the following points:

- Children with different temperaments respond to experiences and interactions differently. What works with one child may not work with another. Therefore, you need to adjust your responses to meet each child's unique needs.

- Although temperament may be inborn, providing appropriate support for children can help them function comfortably. An active child can calm down and a child who tends to withdraw can learn strategies for feeling more comfortable in group situations.

- As you learn the individual temperaments of the children in your care, you may need to adjust your teaching practices, classroom environment, and schedule.

Instruct participants to find a partner. Distribute one description from handout 1B, "Descriptions of Children," to each partnership. Have participants read the description, determine the temperament of the child described, and decide what advice they would offer the teacher.

Refer participants to pages 35–37 in *The Creative Curriculum* for more information on temperamental differences in children.

After most participants are finished, lead a discussion about their work. Read each description and ask volunteers to share their decisions with the group.

Activity 2

Tell participants that now they will have the opportunity to think about their own temperament and to think about how their temperament affects the ways that they understand and respond to various children in their group.

Distribute handout 1C, "Comparing Characteristics of Temperament."

Ask participants to look at each characteristic of temperament and write "me" where they see themselves along the continuum of that characteristic.

After all participants are finished, ask them to think of a child that they work with now or have worked with in the past whose behavior challenged them. Have them think about that child's characteristics of temperament and write the child's initial along each continuum.

When all are finished, ask volunteers to share their results. Make the following points:

- When considering children's behavior, sometimes the behaviors that challenge us the most are those that are closest to our own temperament. Sometimes they challenge us because they are very different from our own.

- Being aware of your own temperaments and those of the children in your group can help you to understand not only children's behaviors but also your reactions to those behaviors.

- For example, if I have a very high sensory threshold, I might have lots of bright colors and bold prints in my classroom. When I look at the continuum for a child whose behavior has been challenging me, I see that she has a low sensory threshold. This might be the cause of her behavior challenges. I can use this new knowledge to tone down my room or make a calm, visually soothing place in the room in which she can relax.

Trainer's Note: This is a good activity to do with teachers when working with them on challenging behaviors. It can help teachers to understand why a certain behavior challenges them and what changes they can make in their teaching practice to better address children's individual temperaments.

Summary

Make the following points:

- Children with different temperaments need to be responded to differently.

- Knowing the temperaments of the children in your care can help you better understand how to support their development and learning.

Notes:

Understanding That Each Child Is Unique: Dual Language

☐ Chart paper
☐ Markers

Preparation

Review pages 39–40 in *The Creative Curriculum*

Take two sheets of chart paper. Label one sheet "Myth" and the other "Reality."

Introduction

Make the following points:

- The number of children in the United States who speak a first language that is not English (English-language learners) or who are learning English at the same time they are learning another language (dual-language learners) has increased dramatically in recent years. This trend is projected to continue.

- Young children in your program may be learning two languages simultaneously: English in your program and another language or languages at home.

- Just as all children have very different strengths and needs, children who are learning English while they are learning another language vary greatly.

- A number of misconceptions about learning two languages can cause unnecessary anxiety for teachers and parents.

Activity

Give the following instructions:

- I am going to read two statements.

- If you believe the statement is true, walk over to the chart labeled "Reality." If you believe the statement is false, walk over to the chart labeled "Myth."

Read the following statements. Lead a short discussion after you read each statement, explaining the reality.

- **Statement**: Children who are exposed to more than one language are at a disadvantage.

  Discussion: This is a myth. Bilingual children often are very creative and good at problem solving. Compared with children who speak one language, bilingual children can communicate with more people, read more, and benefit more from travel. These children also will have an additional skill to offer when they enter the workforce.

- **Statement:** Learning two languages at the same time confuses a young child.

  Discussion: This is a myth. Children do not get confused, even when they are combining languages in one sentence. Mixing languages is a normal and expected part of learning and speaking two languages. In fact, bilingual adults frequently do this, too. This is particularly true for dual-language learners. Infants who hear, babble, and eventually speak two languages use the same part of their brain for both languages, unlike older children and adults who learn a second language.

- **Statement:** When children are exposed to two languages, they can become as proficient in both languages as children who have to master only one language.

  Discussion: This is true. As long as they are exposed consistently to both languages, children can become proficient in both languages.

- **Statement:** Learning two languages as a young child can help children's readiness to read.

  Discussion: This is true. Because they have been exposed to the sounds and letter combinations of two languages, bilingual children's phonological awareness is often better developed than children who have been exposed to only one language.

- **Statement:** Most children have difficulty learning two languages because the process is so complex.

  Discussion: This is a myth. Nearly all children are capable of learning two languages during the early childhood years. While the process may be complex for adults, young children's brains are still developing the structures for language, which enables them to learn multiple languages. After the early childhood years, language structures in the brain are mostly formed. This means that instead of learning a new language, older children and adults can only learn to translate from one language to another—a much more difficult and time-consuming task.

Summary

Make the following points:

- Exposure to rich language experiences in two languages is a definite asset.

- All children can benefit from learning a second language.

Notes:

WORKSHOP

Understanding That Each Child Is Unique: Disabilities

☐ Handout 1D

☐ *The Creative Curriculum*

Preparation

Copy handout 1D, "Strategies for Supporting Children With Disabilities."

Review pages 41–43 in *The Creative Curriculum*.

Introduction

Make the following points:

- *The Creative Curriculum* emphasizes that building trusting relationships is extremely important for young children with disabilities.

- Knowing what support a child needs to be able to participate fully in the program can help you decide what adjustments should be made to, for example, the environment, routines, and experiences.

Activity

Explain that in this activity participants will explore strategies to support children with disabilities.

Distribute handout 1D, "Strategies for Supporting Children With Disabilities." Have participants find a partner.

Give the following instructions:

- Using the index for *The Creative Curriculum*, find sections in the book that offer guidance on meeting the needs of children with disabilities.

- Using handout 1D, record strategies for supporting children with disabilities and where you found each strategy in *The Creative Curriculum*. Also, note how you might use the strategy in your room, what materials you would need, how you would involve families or other staff members, and any other thoughts you have about implementing the strategy.

Give participants 20–30 minutes to work. Ask each partnership to share one strategy with the rest of the group.

Summary

Make the following points:

- All children need to feel included and successful.

- Consider how a specific disability may or may not affect the child's daily life in your program. Use this information to decide what adjustments you need to make, if any, to support a child with that disability.

- *The Creative Curriculum* offers many strategies for supporting children with disabilities and their families.

WORKSHOP

The Goals and Objectives of *The Creative Curriculum®* for Infants, Toddlers & Twos

☐ *The Creative Curriculum,* Appendix, p. 424

Introduction

Make the following points:

- A comprehensive, developmentally appropriate curriculum, like *The Creative Curriculum,* includes goals and objectives for children's learning and development.

- *The Creative Curriculum* goals and objectives outline what children can learn and how they are likely to develop in a quality program.

- Goals and objectives help you to:

  - Focus your ongoing observations and build trusting, caring relationships as you come to appreciate what each child knows and can do.

  - Pay attention to each child's strengths as well as areas in which he or she might need extra support.

  - Decide how to use the information and strategies in *The Creative Curriculum* to make decisions about, for example, the environment, how to build relationships, whether or not to step in, and what to say and do to help individual children develop and learn.

Activity

Refer participants to the goals and objectives in *The Creative Curriculum* and make the following points:

- The goals and objectives of *The Creative Curriculum* address all aspects of a child's development and learning. Four goals define what children are learning: about themselves and others (social/emotional), about moving (physical), about the world (cognitive), and about communicating (language).

- Objectives are delineated for each goal, with a total of 21 objectives.

- The objectives represent a sampling of the knowledge, skills, and behaviors that we hope children will learn in a program that uses *The Creative Curriculum*.

Ask participants to find a partner. Give the following instructions:

- Select one objective from each goal area.

- Think of something that a child might do to demonstrate development for each objective you have selected.

Have volunteers share their examples with the rest of the group.

Summary

Make the following points:

- To provide quality care, you need to know how children develop and what you want them to learn.

- *The Creative Curriculum* goals and objectives address the important aspects of a child's development and learning that can be influenced by your care and teaching.

Looking at Development on a Continuum

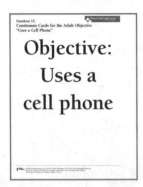

☐ Card stock

☐ Handout 1E

☐ Handout 1F

☐ *The Creative Curriculum,* pp. 45, 47–57

Preparation

Copy handout 1E, "Continuum Cards for the Adult Objective 'Uses a Cell Phone,'" onto card stock.

Copy handout 1F, "Continuum Cards for Goals and Objectives for Infants, Toddlers, and Twos," onto card stock. Cut apart the cards and assemble sets of one copy of each of the steps for each objective. Make enough sets to provide one full set to each table. Shuffle the cards so the objectives and the steps are not in sequence. Place a full set on each table.

Introduction

Introduce the idea of a continuum:

- Goals and objectives define what children should know or be able to do; however, we know that an objective is not achieved all at once.

- Typically, people go through a series of steps when they learn a skill.

Activity 1

Have participants recall the steps they went through when they first learned to use a cell phone.

Ask for six volunteers. Using handout 1E, "Continuum Cards for the Adult Objective 'Uses a Cell Phone,'" give one volunteer the card with the objective. Give each of the others a card describing one of the steps of the objective. Have them read their cards aloud in random order. Then ask them to arrange themselves to depict the correct sequence of steps. Ask the rest of the group if they agree with the order.

Make the following points:

- The steps you outlined are typical steps that most people go through when they learn to use a cell phone.

- Some people may proceed quickly through the steps. Others may progress through the steps at a much slower pace.

- The steps are not defined by age.

- Some people may go beyond Step 5.

- If I were teaching you how to use a cell phone and assessed your progress on a continuum, I would be identifying your strengths, that is, what you could do.

- I would also know the developmental step that follows the step on which you currently are working. I would use that knowledge to plan what I will do to help you progress in learning to use a cell phone. For example, if you could make and receive phone calls, I would plan how to help you learn to check messages on voice mail.

- Now we are going to apply what we have learned to the 21 objectives of *The Creative Curriculum.*

Activity 2

Explain to participants that the purpose of this activity is to become familiar with *The Creative Curriculum® Developmental Continuum for Infants, Toddlers & Twos.*

Give the following directions:

- The set of cards on each table includes the objectives for each of the four goals of *The Creative Curriculum.*

- Each card has the number of a specific objective and one developmental step printed on it.

- First, you are to sort the cards according to objective. Each numbered objective should have five cards.

- Next, put the cards for each objective in the appropriate developmental sequence, from left to right.

As groups finish, refer them to pages 47–57 in *The Creative Curriculum* to identify and discuss any differences between their sequencing and those in the book.

Ask these questions:

- How did you do?

- Did you find any sequencing to be particularly challenging?

- What do you think the benefits of using a continuum might be?

Trainer's Note: Possible responses to the third question are listed on page 46 in *The Creative Curriculum*. You should include in the discussion any advantage listed there that is not mentioned by a participant.

Make the following points:

- Like adults, children do not master a skill or objective all at once. Development typically follows sequential steps.

- The *Developmental Continuum* shows five developmental steps for each of the 21 objectives and gives three increasingly mature examples to illustrate each step.

- The examples of each step are only examples. You may not see the exact behavior because there are so many ways that children show what they know and can do.

Have participants open to page 45 in *The Creative Curriculum*. Review Objective 18, explaining how to read the *Developmental Continuum*.

Summary

Make the following points:

- Knowing how infants, toddlers, and twos develop is the starting point for using *The Creative Curriculum*.

- Knowing infants, toddlers, and twos means appreciating both the general patterns of growth in all children and the many ways that each child is unique.

- Culture influences the way that children develop as well as the way that children demonstrate what they know and can do.

Notes:

Creating a Responsive Environment

Teachers use their knowledge of the social/emotional, physical, cognitive, and language development of infants, toddlers, and twos and their awareness of the many ways in which each child is unique to create an environment that addresses the needs and growing abilities and interests of young children. A well-planned room for infants, toddlers, or twos is a welcoming place for children and families, and a pleasant, efficient place in which to work. As children develop, teachers change the environment to keep children safe, provide new challenges, and inspire new interests. Teachers also use their knowledge of individual children to create schedules, plan for transitions, and complete weekly plans.

Purpose

The following series of workshops addresses the environment in which teachers care for children and welcome families. Through workshop activities, participants evaluate their own room arrangements and consider strategies for selecting and displaying materials. They discover the powerful messages that the physical environment sends to children and families. Participants also explore the ways in which they create a structure for each day.

Big Ideas

Among the important ideas to be learned in this chapter's series of workshops are the following:

- The caregiving environment should include places for daily routines and play experiences.

- A room for infants looks very different from a room for toddlers and twos.

- The toys and materials you make available should promote fine and gross motor skills; be safe for children to explore using all five senses; be appropriate for children's abilities and interests; and provide just the right amount of challenge.

- Materials should be displayed attractively on low shelves that are labeled to show that everything has a place.

- Children's safety and health are primary considerations.

- Some adaptations in the environment may be needed for children with disabilities.

- The daily schedule should be regular enough to be predictable but flexible enough to meet the needs of individual children and respond to unexpected events.

- Planning for infants, toddlers, and twos is planning for possibilities because you can't always predict what will engage and delight a child.

- Responsive planning is a process of documenting what you learn about each child and using that information in planning for each child and for the group.

Creating a Responsive Environment

Workshops

WORKSHOP	KEY POINTS	MATERIALS	TIME (minutes)
Setting Up the Physical Environment (p. 44)	One of the most important ways to put your knowledge of child development into practice is to design spaces that accommodate children's developmental needs, abilities, and interests.	☐ Handout 2A. Space-Planning Guidelines Checklist ☐ *The Creative Curriculum*, pp. 64–73 and 80–83	30
Selecting and Displaying Materials (p. 46)	The materials you select make your environment interesting for young children to explore. If materials are organized and displayed thoughtfully with children's strengths and interests in mind, the children are more likely to use and care for them.	☐ Collection of materials ☐ Handout 2B. Displaying Materials ☐ The *Creative Curriculum*, pp. 74–76	45
Will My Child Be Safe and Healthy? (p. 48)	*The Creative Curriculum* provides specific guidance on what steps you need to take to prevent injuries and provide a healthy environment for young children.	☐ Handout 2C. Will My Child Be Safe and Healthy? ☐ *The Creative Curriculum*, pp. 77–79	60
Messages Conveyed by the Environment (p. 50)	The arrangement of the physical environment sends powerful messages to children and families. It affects how children and adults feel and behave.	☐ Handout 2D. Messages in the Environment ☐ *The Creative Curriculum*, pp. 84–85	30

⬡ WORKSHOP	☍ KEY POINTS	🗎 MATERIALS	⏱ TIME (minutes)
Creating a Schedule (p. 52)	Individual care plans for infants help you keep track of how to handle daily routines for each of the infants in your care. A consistent daily schedule helps toddlers and twos feel more in control and, thus, more competent and secure.	☐ Chart paper ☐ Markers ☐ Handout 2E. Individual Care Plan: Family Information Form ☐ Handout 2F. Individual Care Plan: Family Information Form—Sample ☐ Handout 2G. Individual Care Plans ☐ Handout 2H. Sample Planning Grid for Overall Daily Schedule ☐ *The Creative Curriculum,* pp. 92–93	45
Responsive Planning (p. 58)	Careful observation of what children do and say allows you to reflect on what children are learning and to respond in ways that support each child's development. You can use what you know about the children in your group and about the *Developmental Continuum* as the basis for responsive planning. The "Child Planning Form" and the "Group Planning Form" help you in this process.	☐ Child Planning Form ☐ Group Planning Form ☐ Handout 2I. Completing a Child Planning Form ☐ *The Creative Curriculum,* pp. 47–57 and 97–103	60

WORKSHOP

Setting Up the Physical Environment

☐ Handout 2A

☐ *The Creative Curriculum,* pp. 64–73 and 80–83

Preparation

Ask participants to bring or make floor plans of their own rooms to use as they reflect on the physical environment of a room designed for infants or one designed for toddlers and twos.

Copy handout 2A, "Space-Planning Guidelines Checklist."

Introduction

Make the following points:

- Your knowledge of the social/emotional, physical, cognitive, and language development of infants, toddlers, and twos and of the many ways in which each child is unique enable you to create an environment that addresses the needs and growing abilities and interests of young children.

- Creating a responsive environment is the second component of *The Creative Curriculum.*

Ask participants to think of a store where they hate to shop, that is, a store that drives them crazy. Have them visualize the store: what it looks like, how it smells, what they hear, and how they act and feel when they are shopping there. Ask them to think about what frustrates them as a shopper and what features of the store they really dislike. Allow a few minutes for discussion at the tables. Then ask group members to share their ideas as you record them.

Ask:

- Do these characteristics affect the way you feel and behave?

- Do any of these characteristics apply to rooms for infant, toddler, or twos?

Review the list, drawing parallels between each item and the environment it creates for infants, toddlers, and twos. Discuss how poorly organized environments can make us angry, frustrated, and inefficient, whether we are shopping in a store or working in our program.

Activity

Explain that participants now will compare their floor plans with a checklist of space-planning guidelines.

Distribute handout 2A, "Space-Planning Guidelines Checklist."

Instruct participants to review the checklist and compare it with the floor plan of their room. Have participants refer to pages 64–67 in *The Creative Curriculum* for information on designing spaces for different age groups.

After most participants are finished, ask volunteers to share their findings.

Next, have participants find a partner who works with the same age group that they do.

Tell the partners to read and discuss the sections on pages 67–73 (including the floor plans) and pages 80–83 that apply to the children they work with. Ask them to record, in the "notes" section on handout 2A, any ideas or changes they would like to make to their environments.

Ask volunteers to share their ideas.

Summary

Make the following points:

- A room for infants or for toddlers and twos should have places for all of the routines and experiences.

- One of the most important ways to put your knowledge of child development into practice is to design spaces that accommodate children's developmental needs, abilities, and interests.

- As infants, toddlers, and twos develop and learn, you will need to change the environment to keep children safe, provide new challenges, and inspire new interests.

Selecting and Displaying Materials

☐ Collection of materials

☐ Handout 2B

☐ *The Creative Curriculum,* pp. 74–76

Preparation

Copy handout 2B, "Displaying Materials."

Collect 8–12 pieces of a variety of typical and atypical materials that you might find in a room for infants, toddlers, or twos, such as measuring spoons and cups, lids of different sizes, several mismatched mittens, board books, a doll, interlocking blocks, bean bags, nesting cups, large nontoxic crayons, a wooden puzzle, rattles, fabric samples, a wooden mixing spoon, and a couple of unit blocks. Make sure to include some materials that honor diversity; see page 74 in *The Creative Curriculum* for examples.

Gather enough materials so that each group has its own set of materials, and place a set on each table before starting the workshop.

Introduction

Make the following points:

- The materials you select make your environment interesting for young children to explore.

- If materials are organized and displayed with children's strengths and interests in mind, the children are more likely to use and care for them.

Activity

Assign each table an age group or have each table select the age group that they would like to focus on for this activity.

Give the following instructions:

- Read the description of noncommercial materials on page 74 in *The Creative Curriculum*.

- Sort the materials on your table into two categories: commercial and noncommercial.

When participants are finished sorting, ask:

- What are some examples of how these materials promote children's development and learning?

- How could you involve families in collecting these materials?

Tell each group to select their favorite material from each category and then complete handout 2B, "Displaying Materials." They should refer to pages 74–76 in *The Creative Curriculum* for more information.

Allow 15–20 minutes for the groups to complete this activity. When all the groups are finished, have each share their materials and the ideas they recorded on handout 2B.

Summary

Make the following points:

- When selecting materials, it is important to choose those that gently challenge children's developing abilities, to include materials for a wide range of skills, to include noncommercial materials, and to select materials that honor diversity and the families in your program.

- Store toys and related materials in an area where they will be used most often.

- Display toys using picture and word labels on containers and shelves, so that children can see what is available and choose what they want to play with.

Will My Child Be Safe and Healthy?

☐ Handout 2C
☐ *The Creative Curriculum,* pp. 77–79

Preparation

Review the sections in *The Creative Curriculum* that discuss keeping children safe and healthy. (See the index for relevant pages.)

Introduction

Make the following points:

- Families who are considering group care often worry whether their child will be safe and healthy.

- Safety and health are also primary concerns for anyone taking care of very young children.

Activity

Have participants gather into three groups.

Explain the following:

- In this activity you will learn about the guidance *The Creative Curriculum* offers about keeping infants, toddlers, and twos safe and healthy.

- For the activity, you will be the director of a program serving children under 3 years of age and will be meeting with families who are considering enrolling their child in your program.

- Group 1 will be meeting with the family of an 8-month-old infant; Group 2 will be meeting with the family of a toddler; and Group 3 will be meeting with the family of a 2-year-old.

Give the following instructions:

- The families you are meeting with are very uneasy about placing their children in your program.

- They want to be reassured that their child will be safe and healthy in your care.

- Using pages 77–79 and the index in *The Creative Curriculum,* find suggestions for keeping children of different ages safe and healthy.

- Within your group and using handout 2C, "Will My Child Be Safe and Healthy?" brainstorm what kinds of questions the family might ask.

- List all the things you would say to a family to acknowledge their concerns and reassure them that your program is a safe and healthy place for children.

- Role-play how your meeting would go.

Allow at least 20 minutes for the groups to identify the steps they could take to keep a child safe and healthy and to prepare for their meeting. When they are ready, have each group role-play for the larger group how their meeting would go.

Summary

Make the following points:

- As a teacher or director, you are likely to work with families who will need to be reassured that their child's safety and health will be a primary concern of the program.

- *The Creative Curriculum* provides specific guidance on the steps you need to take to prevent injuries and provide a healthy environment for young children.

- It's also important to find out what policies and procedures your program has established to keep children safe and healthy and to follow those guidelines carefully.

Messages Conveyed by the Environment

☐ Handout 2D

☐ *The Creative Curriculum,* pp. 84–85

Preparation

Copy handout 2D, "Messages in the Environment."

Introduction

Make the following points:

- Have you ever watched children and family members when they first visit your room? They look around to decide what kind of place it is. They may be wondering:

  - Do I belong here?

  - Do these people know who I am? Do they like me?

  - Is this a place I can trust?

  - Will I be safe here?

  - Will I be comfortable here?

  - Can I move around and explore?

  - Is this a calm and interesting place to be?

  - Can I count on these people to take care of me?

- You are the most important part of the learning environment.

- Your daily interactions with the children and families in your care are the most important way to answer these concerns. However, your arrangement of the physical environment also sends powerful messages.

- Teachers who are aware of the power of the physical environment arrange space purposefully to convey five positive messages to children and families. They are:

  - You belong here. We like you.

  - This is a place you can trust. You will be safe here.

  - This is a comfortable place to be.

  - You can move freely and explore on your own.

  - We will take care of you.

Activity

Explain that in this activity, participants will identify ways in which these messages are already conveyed in their rooms and discuss new strategies that they may want to try.

Distribute handout 2D, "Messages in the Environment." Assign one message to each table of participants.

Have participants think of ways in which their current environment communicates their message to the children and families in their programs and record their ideas in column 2 of the handout.

After the groups have finished, have them read about their message in *The Creative Curriculum* (pages 84–85) and write new ideas in column 3 of the handout.

Have each table share their work. Invite other participants to add ideas.

Summary

Make the following points:

- The arrangement of the physical environment sends powerful messages to children and families. It affects how children feel and behave.

- The arrangement of the room and selection of materials convey messages and can support the goals for children's development and learning.

- Take time to regularly assess whether your environment conveys to children that they belong there—that the room is a comfortable place they can trust, that they can move freely and explore on their own, and that they will be cared for—and to consider what changes you want to make.

WORKSHOP

Creating a Schedule

☐ Chart paper
☐ Markers
☐ Handout 2E
☐ Handout 2F
☐ Handout 2G
☐ Handout 2H
☐ *The Creative Curriculum,* pp. 92–93

Preparation

Make enough copies of the following handouts for each group to have a complete set of the seven individual care plans:

- Handout 2E, "Individual Care Plan: Family Information Form"

- Handout 2F, "Individual Care Plan: Family Information Form—Sample"

- Handout 2G, "Individual Care Plans"

- Handout 2H, "Sample Planning Grid for Overall Daily Schedule"

Introduction

Make the following points:

- Each child in your care has his or her own schedule for eating, diapering and toileting, playing, and sleeping.

- In an infant room, each infant is fed when hungry, sleeps in a familiar place when tired, and has his or her diaper changed when wet or soiled. In an infant room, there are as many schedules as there are infants.

- By the time children are toddlers, their days are more consistent and group-oriented. For example, toddlers and twos typically eat and sleep as a group and have designated times for playing.

- A consistent daily schedule helps children feel more in control and, thus, more competent and secure. However, it is still important to be flexible in responding to individual children's needs and to maintain an unhurried pace each day.

Activity 1

Explain that in this activity, participants will review the forms used in creating individual care plans for infants and will practice compiling several plans to create a daily schedule for the children in their group.

Make the following points about handout 2E, "Individual Care Plan: Family Information Form":

- The "Individual Care Plan: Family Information Form" provides information about how the child is cared for at home.

- It includes detailed questions about arrival and departure times, eating and mealtimes, diapering or toileting needs, and sleep habits.

- You complete the form with each child's family when the child enters the program.

- Update the form as the child's care patterns change. At a minimum, review it with families during the family conference.

Review handout 2F, "Individual Care Plan: Family Information Form—Sample," completed for Jasmine.

Make the following points:

- An individual care plan (ICP)

  - Enables you to create a personal schedule for each infant

  - Summarizes information about how best to handle daily routines for an individual child

  - Helps you care for each child in ways that are consistent with the child's home experiences

  - Sends the message to families that you recognize them as experts on their children and that you want to benefit from their knowledge

- It's important to

  - Develop the ICP with the family when the child enters your program

  - Update the plan as the child's care patterns change

  - Keep it where it is accessible to everyone who cares for the child, including substitute teachers

Distribute handout 2G, "Individual Care Plans." Explain to participants that handout 2G includes five completed Individual Care Plans. They will now complete an Individual Care Plan for Jasmine, using the information in the "Individual Care Plan: Family Information Form"

Activity 2

Explain to participants that Individual Care Plans can be compiled to create a daily schedule for an infant room. Distribute handout 2H, "Sample Planning Grid for Overall Daily Schedule," and instruct participants to find a partner. Have them work with their partners to use the information about the six children to create an individualized schedule for the six children in the group.

After most partners have finished, ask them to look at the schedules they created and find times for

- Whole-group or small-group play outdoors

- Individual and small-group play indoors

Ask the groups to now look at their schedules and make some overall statements about the daily schedule for the infants in their group.

Possible responses:

All infants have outdoor time for an hour in the morning and an hour in the afternoon.

All infants are engaged in indoor play experiences throughout the day while they are awake.

All infants are fed when hungry, changed when soiled, and given one-on-one attention.

Bring the whole group back together to discuss their schedules. Ask:

- What was challenging about this process?

- How would this schedule be helpful?

- Who would use this schedule and how would they use it?

Activity 3

Remind participants that by the time children are toddlers and twos, their days are more consistent and group oriented.

Ask participants how a 2-year-old's abilities, needs, and interests are different from those of an infant. Record their responses on chart paper.

Possible responses:

Twos can engage in more extended play.

They are ready to sit with a small group for story.

They have a growing understanding of pictures and words.

They need many opportunities to refine their gross motor skills.

They sometimes need time away from the group.

Ask participants what implications these characteristics have for creating a daily schedule for a group of 2-year-olds. Record their responses on chart paper.

Possible responses:

Include active and quiet times.

Schedule time for outdoor play in the morning and afternoon.

Be aware of children's individual needs for sleeping, toileting, and eating.

Schedule short group times and allow children to decide how long they'd like to stay.

Display an illustrated schedule at children's eye level.

Plan for transitions.

Review the sample schedule for toddlers and twos on pages 92–93 in *The Creative Curriculum.*

Summary

Make the following points:

- The actual times on a daily schedule created from ICPs might change from day to day.

- Even though a schedule might include regular times when children need their diapers changed, diapers should still be checked every hour.

- The schedule can help you and your co-teachers coordinate responsibilities.

- It can also help you decide when to provide experiences (indoors and outdoors) for children who are awake and not eating or having their diapers changed.

- A consistent daily schedule helps toddlers and twos feel more in control and thus more competent and secure.

- However, it is still important to be flexible about responding to individual children's needs and to maintain an unhurried pace each day.

Notes:

Responsive Planning

☐ Child Planning Form
☐ Group Planning form
☐ Handout 21
☐ *The Creative Curriculum,* pp. 45–57 and 97–103

Preparation

Copy handout 21, "Completing a Child Planning Form," and gather copies of the "Child Planning Form" and the "Group Planning Form."

Introduction

Make the following points:

- Responsive planning is an important part of creating a responsive environment that addresses the needs, interests, and abilities of the children in your care.

- As you work with infants, toddlers, and twos, you continually observe what they are doing and saying. Think about what you learn about each child and respond in supportive ways.

- Referring to the *Developmental Continuum* and keeping the goals and objectives in mind as you observe children will help you think about what you see and hear, decide how to respond at that moment, and plan later for each child and the entire group.

Activity 1

Explain the following:

- Now that you understand how to create a schedule for infants, toddlers, and twos, you can consider weekly planning for individual children and the group.

- When you observe children throughout the day, using the *Developmental Continuum* to guide your observations, you will learn a lot about a child's development.

- Using this knowledge, you can individualize strategies and activities that support each child's development.

- This next activity focuses on how to use what you know about each child and what you know from the *Developmental Continuum* to plan for individual children and the group.

- Look at the *Developmental Continuum* on pages 47–57 in *The Creative Curriculum*.

  - Choose three objectives.

  - For each developmental step, write a suggested activity or strategy to support children's development.

Offer the following examples:

- **Objective 1**: Trusts known, caring adults

  Step 1: Recognizes and reaches out to familiar adults

  Strategy: Assign primary caregivers so children learn who they can trust to meet their needs and care for them.

- **Objective 1**: Trusts known, caring adults

  Step 5: Functions with increasing comfort in a variety of environments, relying on connections to familiar adults who are not immediately present

  Activity: Ask families to bring in family photos and invite children to help create a class book of family pictures.

After the groups have finished, have each share an objective and the related strategies or activities that they discussed.

Activity 2

Have participants open to page 97 in *The Creative Curriculum*. Discuss the "Child Planning Form."

Explain the following to participants:

- To offer an individualized program, you need to know and appreciate what makes each child special. When you understand what motivates a child, how the child approaches new tasks, and what his or her preferred learning style is, you can plan for that child.

- Two forms will help you plan and individualize your program for children: the "Child Planning Form" and the "Group Planning Form." Copies of these forms can be found in the *Developmental Continuum Assessment Toolkit* and online for CreativeCurriculum.net subscribers.

- Weekly planning is important because it sets the stage for meaningful experiences and gives you an overall sense of direction for the week.

- Each week, you will take a few minutes to review your observation notes and portfolio items and to reflect on recent events, interactions, and what you have learned about each child in your primary care group.

- You may ask yourself questions such as:

  - Has this child demonstrated any new accomplishments or shown any new interests, likes, or dislikes?

  - Is there any family news or a special need that I need to consider?

- You will record your reflections on the "Child Planning Form" in the "current information" section.

- Next, you will write down how you will use your current reflections to promote the development of that child in the coming week. You will record your ideas in the section labeled "plans." For example, plans might include making changes to routines, introducing new materials, and so forth.

Distribute the handout 21, "Completing a Child Planning Form."

Ask participants to review the handout and then to work in pairs to complete the form for Maria, Aaliyah, and Justin.

Ask volunteers to share their ideas with the group.

Activity 3

Have participants turn to page 100 in *The Creative Curriculum*.

Explain the following:

- Weekly planning for a group of infants, toddlers, and twos can be thought of as planning for possibilities.

- To plan for your group, examine the information recorded about the individual children on their "Child Planning Form" and then decide what changes need to be made to the environment (including materials), routines, and the schedule. Write down any special experiences you plan to offer during the week, such as opportunities to explore and make discoveries, to enjoy stories and songs, and to participate in art or cooking activities.

- You might find it helpful to reflect on the previous week. You may ask yourself questions such as:

  - What experiences interested the children?

  - Which materials did the children use?

  - What skills did the children demonstrate?

  - What worked well? What problems came up?

  - How did we provide meaningful roles for family members who visited the program?

- In the "family involvement" section of the form, you will write down ways to involve families, such as asking them for help in making materials or inviting them to participate in an activity or daily routine.

- In the "thoughts for next week" section of the form, you will record how well you think your current week has worked. Include information on how engaged the children were, what actually happened, and what changes you want to make for the following week.

Distribute the "Group Planning Form."

Have participants work in pairs or small groups to complete the "Group Planning Form" for the group of children described on the "Child Planning Form." Encourage them to refer to pages 98–100 in *The Creative Curriculum*. Also suggest that they look in the eight experiences chapters, in Part 3, for ideas they can use in completing the "Group Planning Form."

Bring the group back together and invite each pair or group to share.

Using pages 101–103 in *The Creative Curriculum*, review the process that LaToya and her assistant teacher went through to complete their weekly planning.

Explain the following:

- The box on page 101 describes how a teacher can expand on children's interests by incorporating several different experiences in the weekly plan. In the example, LaToya and her assistant teacher use their observation notes to reflect on the children's current interests and also considered the developmental skills of the children in their group.

- Page 102 shows how LaToya recorded the children's interests on her "Child Planning Form." She and her assistant used this information to brainstorm ways to extend children's interest in leaves in several different experiences throughout the week.

- On page 103, they incorporate their ideas into the "Group Planning Form."

Summary

Summarize with the following points:

- As you work with young children, you must carefully observe what children do and say so that you can reflect on what children are learning and respond in ways that support each child's development.

- You can use what you know about the children in your group and about the *Developmental Continuum* as the basis for responsive planning.

- The "Child Planning Form" and the "Group Planning Form" help you in this process.

- When you work with infants, toddlers, and twos, you must always expect the unexpected. Each infant has a personal schedule and style.

- Being responsive is more important than accomplishing particular activities or sticking to a plan.

- Review group planning forms and adapt plans to meet the children's changing needs and interests.

What Children Are Learning

Every interaction a child experiences and every impression a child forms by seeing, tasting, touching, smelling, and hearing affects the development of that child's brain and builds new abilities. What and how children learn during the first 3 years become the building blocks for successful lifelong learning. Children develop their understanding of language and literacy, math, and science more readily when they have positive, trusting relationships with the important adults in their lives. The relationships that teachers build with children and the experiences teachers provide for them build the foundation for school success.

Purpose

The following workshops explore the social/emotional characteristics and attitudes that influence the way children learn. Through workshop activities, participants learn strategies for supporting children's learning in language and literacy, math, and science.

Big Ideas

The important ideas conveyed in this chapter's series of workshops include the following:

- Children who enter school ready to learn have strong social/emotional skills and positive attitudes towards learning. They demonstrate confidence, curiosity, intentionality, self-control, relatedness, the capacity to communicate, and an ability to cooperate with others. All of these skills and attitudes can be nurtured during the first 3 years of life.

- To promote language and literacy development, teachers talk with children during daily routines and experiences to build their vocabulary and language skills; engage children in songs, poems, fingerplays, and stories that expose them to the sounds and rhythms of language; read books with children and tell them stories every day; and provide opportunities for children to explore writing.

- To encourage children to discover mathematical relationships, teachers use numbers in songs and rhymes. To teach number concepts, teachers provide experiences in comparing sizes and amounts. They point out patterns in the environment, encourage children to recognize shapes and positions in space, and provide materials that children can organize and sort.

- To support children's curiosity about the world, teachers provide opportunities for children to explore like scientists. They provide safe objects and materials for children to manipulate, taste, shake, and observe; take children outdoors to explore nature; and talk about the different people in their world and the work they do.

What Children Are Learning

Workshops

⬡ WORKSHOP	⚲ KEY POINTS	▤ MATERIALS	⏲ TIME (minutes)
The Foundation for All Learning (p. 68)	Social/emotional skills and a positive approach to learning are the base upon which infants, toddlers, and twos build cognitive and language skills and acquire knowledge about the world around them.	☐ Chart paper ☐ Markers ☐ *The Creative Curriculum,* pp. 108–109	45
Sharing Your Expertise (p. 72)	From infancy, children are building their language and literacy skills, discovering mathematical relationships, and exploring like scientists.	☐ Handout 3A. What Children Are Learning ☐ *The Creative Curriculum,* chapter 3	60
Two Stories About Learning (p. 74)	It is important for teachers to provide experiences to support children's learning that not only relate to language and literacy, math, and science but also support the seven characteristics that are essential to children's success as learners.	☐ Handout 3B. Teaching and Learning: Two Stories ☐ Handout 3C. Two Stories Thought Sheet ☐ *The Creative Curriculum,* chapter 3	45–60
Collections for Learning (p. 76)	By purposefully using materials that are readily available in infant, toddler, and twos rooms, teachers can support children's learning in language and literacy, math, and science.	☐ Balls ☐ Lids ☐ Noise-Making toys ☐ Books ☐ Handout 3D. Collections for Learning ☐ *The Creative Curriculum,* chapter 3	60–75

⬡ WORKSHOP	⚷ KEY POINTS	▤ MATERIALS	⏱ TIME (minutes)
Connecting Content With Routines and Experiences (p. 78)	Infants, toddlers, and twos build language and literacy skills, discover mathematical relationships, and explore like scientists during the eight play experiences in *The Creative Curriculum*.	☐ Sticky notes: 3" x 5," two colors ☐ Square sticky notes, 3" x 3" ☐ Chart paper ☐ Markers ☐ Handout 3E. Content and Experiences ☐ *The Creative Curriculum,* chapters 11–18	60

The Foundation for All Learning

☐ Chart paper

☐ Markers

☐ *The Creative Curriculum,* pp. 108–109

Preparation

Read pages 108–109 in *The Creative Curriculum.*

Introduction

Make the following points:

- The third component of *The Creative Curriculum* addresses what children are learning.

- Every interaction and every impression a child receives by seeing, tasting, touching, smelling, and hearing affects the development of the child's brain and builds new abilities.

- What and how children learn during the first 3 years become the building blocks for successful, lifelong learning.

- The relationships you build with children and the experiences you provide to them build the foundation for school success.

Activity

Go through the following interactive mini-lecture.

- School readiness is a very important issue today. Children who enter school ready to learn have strong social/emotional skills and positive attitudes toward learning.

- How children feel about themselves and how they relate to others influence what and how they learn.

- Ask: "Why do people say that school readiness begins in infancy?" Discuss participant responses.

- ZERO TO THREE: National Center for Infants, Toddlers, and Families identifies seven social/emotional characteristics essential for school readiness.[1] They are:

  - Confidence: a person's sense of control over his or her own behavior and environment; children's expectation that they will be able to succeed and that adults will help them if necessary

  - Curiosity: a desire to find things out, knowing the process will be enjoyable

  - Intentionality: the drive to make things happen and a determination to persist and not give up

  - Self-Control: children's ability to control their actions in age-appropriate ways

  - Relatedness: children's ability to engage with others, knowing they will be understood

  - Capacity to communicate: the desire and ability to exchange ideas, feelings, and thoughts with others

  - Cooperativeness: children's ability to engage with others in an activity or task, balancing their own needs with those of others to accomplish something

- Young children develop these characteristics when they are with adults who genuinely care about them, talk with them in calm and respectful ways, take joy in their discoveries, have appropriate expectations about what they can do, and guide their behavior in positive ways.

Have participants form seven groups. Assign each group one of the seven characteristics and give each group a sheet of chart paper and set of markers.

---

[1] **Zero to Three.** (1992) *Heart Start: The emotional foundations of school readiness.* Retrieved February 7, 2006, from http://www.zerotothree.org/sch_read.html

Give the following instructions:

- Divide your chart into two sections.

- In one section, record examples of how infants, toddlers, and twos demonstrate your group's assigned characteristic.

- In the other section, record ideas about what teachers can do to cultivate it.

- Feel free to use pictures, words, and symbols to convey your ideas.

- Use pages 108–109 in *The Creative Curriculum* to get ideas. Be sure to include your own ideas in addition to those presented in the book.

After 15–20 minutes, have each small group present their chart to the rest of the participants.

Summary

Make the following points:

- School readiness begins in infancy.

- Social/emotional skills and a positive attitude toward learning are the base upon which infants, toddlers, and twos develop cognitive and language skills and acquire knowledge about the world around them.

- Children develop these skills when they have secure attachments to the important people in their lives: their families and teachers.

Notes:

Sharing Your Expertise

☐ Handout 3A

☐ *The Creative Curriculum,* chapter 3

Preparation

Copy handout 3A, "What Children Are Learning."

Introduction

Make the following points:

- When children feel secure and loved, they are eager to explore and learn about the world around them.

- From birth, young children begin developing language and literacy skills. They are communicators, eager to let you know what they need and think.

- Young children think mathematically, comparing who has more, putting things in order by size, noticing different shapes, matching, and sorting.

- They are also scientists, examining and manipulating everything that comes within reach to try to figure how things work, how they grow, and what people do.

Activity

Explain that in this activity, participants will have the opportunity to develop expertise in a specific content area of learning.

Have participants count off by 11.

Assign the following topics to the numbers:

1. Vocabulary and language

2. The sounds and rhythms of language

3. Enjoying stories and books

4. Exploring writing

5. Number concepts

6. Patterns and relationships

7. Geometry and spatial relationships

8. Sorting and classifying

9. The physical world

10. The natural world

11. The social world

Distribute handout 3A, "What Children Are Learning."

Explain to participants that they will read the section in chapter 3 of *The Creative Curriculum* that discusses their assigned area of learning and become our session experts on the topic, specifically by understanding what the content area is about, how children demonstrate their learning in this area, and what teachers can do to support children's learning. They can record their thoughts on handout 3A.

Give participants enough time to read and make notes about their topic. After everyone is done, give the following instructions:

- You will now be able to share your expertise with others.

- Circulate around the room, find session experts in different content areas, and share your knowledge.

- Make notes about what you learn about each content area from the other session experts.

Pull the group together and ask if anyone wants to share what they learned from this activity.

Summary

Make the following points:

- From infancy, children are building their language and literacy skills, discovering mathematical relationships, and exploring like scientists.

- Children show their learning in many ways.

- You can do and say many different things to support and encourage children's learning.

Two Stories About Learning

☐ Handout 3B

☐ Handout 3C

☐ *The Creative Curriculum,* chapter 3

Preparation

Copy handout 3B, "Teaching and Learning: Two Stories," and handout 3C, "Two Stories Thought Sheet."

Introduction

Make the following points:

- You encourage children's learning when you provide experiences that support children's confidence, curiosity, intentionality, self-control, relatedness, capacity to communicate, and cooperativeness.

- Every interaction you have with a child is an opportunity to nurture these seven characteristics.

Activity

Tell participants that they will now have the opportunity to consider what children are learning by examining two different teacher's approaches to learning experiences.

Distribute handouts 3B, "Teaching and Learning: Two Stories," and 3C, "Two Stories Thought Sheet."

Have participants work with the others at their table to read each scenario and answer the questions on handout 3C:

- What do you think the teacher wanted the children to learn?

- How does this teacher think children learn?

- How does the teacher spend her time?

- How do the children spend their time?

- What did the children learn?

Encourage participants to reference chapter 3 of *The Creative Curriculum* and to consider the content areas as well as the seven characteristics that are essential for school readiness.

After most tables are finished, lead a large-group discussion about their findings.

Summary

Make the following points:

- Children are learning all the time.

- Meaningful experiences support children's learning in language and literacy, math, and science and also support the seven characteristics that are essential to children's success as learners.

Collections for Learning

- ☐ Balls
- ☐ Lids
- ☐ Noise-Making toys
- ☐ Books
- ☐ Handout 3D
- ☐ *The Creative Curriculum*, chapter 3

Preparation

Gather enough balls, lids, noise-making toys (such as rattles, shakers, bells, and small drums), and books so that each table will have one collection of like items.

Place one collection on each table; for example, place the collection of balls on one table and all of the books on another table.

Copy handout 3D, "Collections for Learning."

Trainer's Note: The toys in the collections should be appropriate for all infants, toddlers, and twos.

Introduction

Make the following points:

- As infants, toddlers, and twos explore their environments and play, they are acquiring skills and knowledge in language and literacy, mathematical relationships, and science concepts.

- Everyday materials can provide wonderful learning opportunities for young children.

Activity

Tell participants that in this activity they will consider what children are learning and how teachers can support children's learning by exploring a collection of objects.

Distribute handout 3D, "Collections for Learning."

Have participants explore their collections and, as a group, complete the chart on handout 3D.

Encourage participants to use chapter 3 of *The Creative Curriculum* as a resource.

After all tables are finished, ask volunteers to share their collection and findings with the whole group.

Summary

Make the following points:

- Collections of everyday materials can be wonderful learning materials for young children.

- By purposefully using materials that are readily available in infant, toddler, and twos rooms, teachers can support children's learning in language and literacy, math, and science.

Connecting Content With Routines and Experiences

☐ Sticky notes: 3" x 5," two colors

☐ Square sticky notes, 3" x 3"

☐ Chart paper

☐ Markers

☐ Handout 3E

☐ *The Creative Curriculum,* chapters 11–18

Preparation

Review chapter 3 and all experiences chapters in *The Creative Curriculum.*

Tape several pieces of chart paper together and make a large chart that looks like handout 3E, "Content and Experiences." Post it on the wall.

Introduction

Make the following points:

- Infants, toddlers, and twos build language and literacy skills, discover mathematical relationships, and explore like scientists throughout the day.

- The eight play experiences in *The Creative Curriculum* offer many opportunities for children to explore and learn.

Activity

Give the following instructions:

- Tell participants that they are going to do an activity that will help them appreciate how content connects with experiences.

- Divide the group in half. Tell one half of the group that they will represent one of the eight play experiences in *The Creative Curriculum;* tell the other half of the group that they will represent the content areas of literacy, mathematics, and science.

- Invite each participant in the experiences group to pick out an experience they want to explore further. Invite the participants in the other group to select language and literacy, mathematical relationships, the physical world, the natural world, or the social world. (Make sure that each experience and content area has at least one representative; recruit a volunteer for any experience or area that is not represented.)

- Refer participants to the appropriate experience chapter in *The Creative Curriculum* and ask them to take about 5 minutes to review it.

- Using one color of sticky notes, have all of the participants representing experiences write the name of their experience on a sticky note. Invite them to place the note on their chest, forehead, or other place where it will be visible. Using the second color of sticky note, invite the content group to do the same with the name of their content area.

- Give a signal for all participants to walk around the room, carrying a pad of square sticky notes, a pencil or pen, and, if they want it, their book.

- Invite them to mingle and find a person with the opposite color note. Together, on their square sticky notes, they should write down an idea about how their experience and content area support each other.

- As each pair finishes, they should go to the large chart and put their sticky note in the appropriate section.

- Have participants continue circulating so that they pair up several times.

Allow 25–30 minutes for this activity. Review the wall chart, noticing areas where there are many ideas and areas where there are fewer ideas. Invite participants to add ideas to any empty places on the chart.

Summary

Make the following points:

- Everyday experiences offer opportunities for children to develop and learn.

- The eight play experiences in *The Creative Curriculum* help you plan appropriate and rich learning experiences for young children.

Trainer's Note: This workshop can be used when you are doing training on either "What Children Are Learning" or "Introduction to All Experiences." You can also adapt the workshop to show how the five daily routines support building language and literacy, discovering mathematical relationships, and exploring like scientists.

Caring and Teaching

Caring for and teaching infants, toddlers, and twos is interesting, fun, joyful, rewarding, and sometimes challenging and exhausting. Appreciating and finding joy in the everyday discoveries that delight a child make teaching children under age 3 satisfying and enjoyable. As teachers observe and get to know each child, they reflect and respond to individual strengths, needs, and interests; purposefully guide behavior; support learning; and use ongoing assessment to document each child's progress and to plan.

Purpose

This workshop series explores the many roles of the teacher. Participants learn strategies for building relationships with children and for guiding their behavior. Participants are also introduced to the ongoing cycle of observing, guiding children's learning, and assessing children's progress by using *The Creative Curriculum® Developmental Continuum for Infants, Toddlers & Twos.*

Big Ideas

The important ideas to be learned in this chapter's workshops include these:

- Very young children flourish when they have close, supportive, and trusting relationships with the important adults in their lives.

- A positive relationship with a primary caregiver makes children feel safe enough to explore, try new things, experiment, and learn.

- Teachers support children's development by keeping group sizes small, creating a calm atmosphere, and purposefully helping children learn to get along with others and develop positive social skills.

- Self-regulation, the ability to control one's own feelings and behaviors, is a primary task of early childhood. Teachers need patience and understanding as well as skills in using a variety of strategies to guide children's behavior.

- Teachers guide children's learning by taking an interest in what fascinates them, talking with them about their experiences, and extending their ideas. Teachers also provide extra support for children who are learning more than one language or who have a disability.

- Ongoing assessment is the process of gathering and analyzing information about children. Teachers use *The Creative Curriculum Developmental Continuum for Infants, Toddlers & Twos* Assessment System to document their observations, analyze what they have learned, and plan for each child and for the group.

Caring and Teaching

Workshops

⚙ WORKSHOP	🔑 KEY POINTS	📄 MATERIALS	⏱ TIME (minutes)
How Is a Teacher Like …? (p. 84)	Effective teachers play many different roles as they care for a group of children and build relationships with each child.	☐ 8½" x 11" paper ☐ Handout 4A. How Is a Teacher Like…? ☐ *The Creative Curriculum,* p. 137	20
Building a Relationship With Each Child (p. 86)	Teachers use a variety of strategies to build a trusting relationship with each child in their care.	☐ Chart paper ☐ Markers ☐ *The Creative Curriculum,* pp. 138–144	30
Helping Children Get Along With Others (p. 92)	Teachers use many different strategies for helping children get along with others and manage life in a group setting.	☐ Chart paper ☐ Markers and scissors ☐ Handout 4B. Strategies for Helping Children Get Along With Others ☐ *The Creative Curriculum,* pp. 22–26 and 141–142	45
Using Positive Guidance Strategies (p. 94)	Many positive guidance strategies are available that teachers can use to prevent, minimize, and respond to unwanted behaviors.	☐ Chart paper ☐ Markers ☐ Card stock or other heavyweight paper ☐ Handout 4C. Is This Positive Guidance? ☐ Handout 4D. Positive Guidance Strategies ☐ Handout 4E. Positive Guidance Cube ☐ *The Creative Curriculum,* pp. 146–152	60

⬡ WORKSHOP	⚷ KEY POINTS	🗐 MATERIALS	🕐 TIME (minutes)
Guiding Children's Learning: Talking With Infants, Toddlers, and Twos (p. 100)	Through verbal and nonverbal exchanges, teachers help children to make sense of their world, express and think about new ideas, stretch their thinking, and expand their vocabulary development; and show children that they care about them.	☐ Baskets (enough for each table to have one) ☐ Handout 4F. Talking With Infants, Toddlers, and Twos to Guide Their Learning ☐ *The Creative Curriculum,* p. 163	30
Challenging Behaviors (p. 102)	Temper tantrums and biting are two of the most common challenging behaviors. Observation and talking with families can help you determine the cause of, prevent, and respond to challenging behaviors.	☐ Chart paper ☐ Handout 4G. Temper Tantrums ☐ Handout 4H. Why Children Sometimes Bite ☐ *The Creative Curriculum*, pp. 155–158	90
Assessing Children's Development and Learning: An Overview (p. 108)	As teachers observe and get to know children, they use ongoing assessment to document children's progress; to plan experiences that meet their needs, interests, and abilities; and to talk with families about their child's development and learning.	☐ 8½" x 11" paper for each participant ☐ Markers ☐ "Family Conference Form" ☐ "Individual Child Profile" booklets ☐ Handout 4I. Linking Curriculum and Assessment: The Ongoing Cycle ☐ Handout 4J. Sample Observation Notes ☐ Handout 4K. Year at a Glance ☐ *The Creative Curriculum*, pp. 47–57, 169–170, 175, and Appendix, p. 424, "Goals and Objectives at a Glance"	45

How Is a Teacher Like …?

☐ 8½" x 11" paper

☐ Handout 4A

☐ *The Creative Curriculum,* p. 137

Preparation

Copy handout 4A, "How Is a Teacher Like…?"

Introduction

- "Caring and Teaching," the fourth component of *The Creative Curriculum,* examines the many different aspects of your role.

- While the teacher's role is a part of every chapter and every workshop, this series of activities will focus exclusively on how you use your knowledge of child development, individual children, and content to guide children's development and learning.

Activity

Distribute handout 4A, "How Is a Teacher Like…?"

Assign each table one profession and provide the following instructions:

- Discuss how the work of a teacher is similar to the assigned profession. Give specific examples.

- Record your ideas in the appropriate space on the handout.

- Prepare to share your ideas.

Have the groups share key points from their group discussions. Invite them to suggest other job descriptions that might be similar to the teacher's role.

Have participants read page 137 in *The Creative Curriculum.*

Summary

Make the following points:

- You have many roles as a teacher.

- Like the gardener, you care for and nurture the children in your room, continually assessing their growth and making changes to meet their needs.

- Like the coach, you guide children's learning and behavior in positive ways to achieve positive outcomes for all children.

- Like the air traffic controller, you must keep track of what each child is doing at all times and coordinate the daily routines and experiences so that everything goes smoothly and individual needs are met.

- And like an architect, you design a warm, welcoming, and appropriate environment for the children in your care and ensure that it works as intended.

Building a Relationship With Each Child

☐ Chart paper

☐ Markers

☐ *The Creative Curriculum,* pp. 138–144

Preparation

Review pages 138–144 in *The Creative Curriculum.*

Introduction

Make the following points:

- The importance of building responsive relationships is an underlying theme in *The Creative Curriculum.*

- Every interaction you have with children is an opportunity to build relationships that help them thrive.

- You can use many strategies to help children get along with others and manage life in a group setting.

- Program policies and procedures can support the building of trusting, responsive relationships with children.

Activity 1

Explain to participants that in this activity they will be asked to close their eyes and visualize something while you are talking.

Trainer's Note: "Guided imagery" is an exercise in which participants sit comfortably, close their eyes, and reflect silently on what is being read aloud to them. When reading a guided imagery, it is helpful to read slowly and in a calm, comforting, and steady voice. Pause at times to allow participants to create mental pictures and come up with answers to questions while you are reading. Some people may experience strong feelings during this exercise. Be sure to pay attention to people's reactions while you are reading the story so you can help anyone who may feel upset. Offer the option of not participating if any participant feels uncomfortable.

Give the following instructions slowly, in a quiet voice:

- Sit comfortably in your chair and close your eyes.

- Imagine that you are traveling in another country where they do not speak your language.

- You have been in an accident and are taken to the hospital.

- In the hospital, you awaken and discover that you are unable to move easily. You need help to go to the bathroom, to eat, to reposition your body in bed, and to get dressed. No one in the hospital speaks your language so you are unable to communicate to the staff with words.

- Because your fine motor skills are impaired, you cannot draw pictures to communicate.

- Develop a clear picture in your mind of what this would be like.

- How do you feel about this situation?

- What are your concerns?

- What could the nurses and doctors in the hospital do to help you feel comfortable?

- What could they do to make you trust them?

- Keeping these thoughts with you, when you are ready, open your eyes.

Invite participants to share their thoughts with the other members of their group. Then ask volunteers to share with the whole group their thoughts of how they would like the doctors and nurses to treat them in the imagined scenario.

Possible responses:

Be respectful.

Treat gently.

Meet needs promptly.

Use a soothing tone of voice.

Smile, talk, and try to communicate.

Be responsive to attempts to communicate through facial expressions and tone.

Be kind.

Follow the same routine so care is predictable.

Have consistent caregivers.

Find ways to give choices so I don't feel powerless.

Be reassuring.

Ask the group what the relationship is between their imagined experience at the hospital with the doctors and nurses and the experience that infants, toddlers, and twos have with their caregivers and teachers. Record their ideas on the same chart paper.

Possible responses:

Infants, toddlers, and twos want to be treated in the same ways we wanted to be treated by the doctors and nurses.

We should treat children gently and meet their needs promptly.

Use a soothing tone of voice.

Smile, talk, and try to communicate.

Be responsive to attempts to communicate through facial expressions and tone.

Be kind.

Follow the same routine so care is predictable.

Have consistent teachers.

Find ways to give infants and toddlers choices so they don't feel powerless.

Write "Building Trust" at the top of the chart on which you recorded participants' responses. Explain that establishing and maintaining a trusting, caring relationship with the children in their care are all teachers' primary responsibilities. Highlight the following practices (adding them to the list if necessary):

- Respond promptly to infants' cries to teach them that they can trust you and to help them to see themselves as competent individuals who can affect the world around them.

- Assign primary caregivers so children learn on whom they can rely to meet their needs.

- Use your face, voice, touch, and motion to help children manage or regulate stimulation and feelings.

- Use caring words to let children know that they are respected, understood, and valued.

- Offer children opportunities to make decisions, whenever possible.

- Establish and follow rituals and routines, providing as much continuity with a child's home as possible.

- Maintain positive relationships and teamwork among the adults in the room so that a positive tone is set for relationships with children. When adults don't get along, children sense the tension.

Have participants review the section "Strategies for Building Trusting Relationships" on pages 138–140 in *The Creative Curriculum*.

Activity 2

Ask participants to turn to pages 143–144 in *The Creative Curriculum*. Review the section "A Structure That Supports Relationships," making the following points:

- Program policies and procedures can help support trusting, responsive relationships with children.

- Small group sizes allow teachers to interact with children individually, take the time needed for daily routines, observe and respond to each child, and follow the child's lead.

- The National Association for the Education of Young Children has recommendations for group sizes and teacher-child ratios for programs caring for infants, toddlers, and twos.

- A primary caregiver has the major responsibility for a child's care and education. A relationship with a primary caregiver helps children feel secure and able to explore and learn.

- Continuity of care refers to a program philosophy that supports children's staying with the same teacher for all—or at least most—of their first 3 years. Programs can promote continuity of care in several ways.

Summary

Make the following points:

- Many of the same practices that would help you build trust also apply to what young children need to develop a trusting relationship with you.

- Use every opportunity to develop a relationship with each child and to nurture the child's trust in you.

- Consider whether the policies in your program support relationships and, if not, what changes might be possible.

Notes:

Helping Children Get Along With Others

☐ Chart paper
☐ Markers
☐ Scissors
☐ Handout 4B
☐ *The Creative Curriculum,* pp. 22–26 and 141–142

Preparation

Review pages 140–142 in *The Creative Curriculum.*

Make one copy of handout 4B, "Strategies for Helping Children Get Along With Others," and cut the statements into strips.

Label four sheets of chart paper with one of the following headings: young infants, mobile infants, toddlers, and twos. Hang the sheets on the walls around the room. Place a set of markers near each chart.

Introduction

Make the following points:

• The trusting relationship you build with each child helps form the foundation for their other relationships.

• When you treat children in loving, respectful, and consistent ways, you promote their positive attitudes toward others.

• Even with all of your support, life in group care can be stressful for children.

• You can use many strategies to help children get along with each other and manage life in a group setting.

Activity

Distribute a couple of the strategies that you cut into strips to each group. Give the following instructions:

• With the people at your table, read the strategies you've been given for helping children get along with others.

• For each strategy, decide if it is appropriate for young infants, mobile infants, toddlers, or twos. A strategy may be appropriate for more than one age group.

• For a detailed description of your strategies, refer to pages 141–142 in *The Creative Curriculum* for more information.

• When you have made your decision, record your strategies on the appropriate chart for the age group or groups that you have selected. Use the markers that have been placed by each chart.

After the groups have finished, have participants sit by the chart of the age group that they would like to continue to work on. If no one is sitting by a chart, ask volunteers to switch so at least one person is sitting by each chart. Give the following instructions:

- With the people in your group, brainstorm other specific, age-appropriate strategies that you can use to help children get along with others.

- You may want to refer to pages 22–26 of *The Creative Curriculum* for information about children's social/ emotional development for your age group.

After 15 minutes, invite groups to present their charts to the rest of the participants.

Summary

Make the following points:

- Use a variety of strategies help children get along with each other and manage life in a group setting.

- Understanding the social/emotional development of each age group will help you decide which strategies are appropriate for the children in your care.

- Having a calm atmosphere and small group sizes are important ways to create a positive social environment.

- Modeling appropriate behaviors, providing multiples of favorite toys, acknowledging children's positive interactions, and encouraging children to help one another are all ways that you help them build relationships with each other.

Using Positive Guidance Strategies

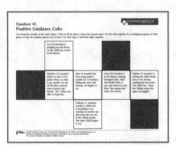

- ☐ Chart paper
- ☐ Markers
- ☐ Card stock or other heavyweight paper
- ☐ Handout 4C
- ☐ Handout 4D
- ☐ Handout 4E
- ☐ *The Creative Curriculum,* pp. 146–152

Preparation

Hang a sheet of chart paper in the front of the room.

Copy handout 4C, "Is This Positive Guidance?" handout 4D, "Positive Guidance Strategies," and (on cardstock) handout 4E, "Positive Guidance Cube." Make enough copies of handout 4C, "Is This Positive Guidance?" so that each group of 4–6 participants has a copy.

Cut out the figures in handout 4E, "Positive Guidance Cube," and assemble them into cubes. Follow the assembly directions on the handout.

Introduction

Make the following points:

- Self-regulation is one of the important developmental tasks of the early childhood years.

- Having a variety of positive guidance strategies will enable you to help children develop increasing control over their feelings and behavior.

Activity 1

Introduce the activity by telling participants that they will observe you interacting with a child in two different ways. Instruct them to observe your interactions.

Ask a volunteer, who is comfortable pretending to cry, to come to the front of the room.

Tell the group that the volunteer participant is a toddler who has just spilled her macaroni and cheese on the floor and is starting to cry.

Say to the participant in an annoyed voice as you roll your eyes:

> *Oh, not again. You always spill things. When will you learn? Get a paper towel and start cleaning it up. I'm not doing it for you. And would you stop your crying?*

Ask the group for reactions to the interaction. Ask questions such as:

- How do you think that child feels?

- What did the child learn from the teacher?

Tell the group that they will now see the teacher respond differently to the same situation.

Say to the volunteer in a compassionate voice as you gently touch her shoulder:

> *It is frustrating when things get spilled. You are really hungry and I know how much you love macaroni and cheese. I can help you clean it up and then we can get you some more. See, there's lots of macaroni left (as you point to an imaginary bowl). Would you like to use the paper towels or the sponge to clean up?*

Ask for reactions to the second interaction using the same questions as before.

- How do you think that child feels?

- What did the child learn from the teacher?

Make the following points:

- Young children are developing self-regulation, the ability to control their feelings and behavior.

- Infants, toddlers, and twos have immediate and intense feelings of joy and excitement, as well as feelings of anger and frustration.

- They do not yet have the ability to stop and think about how to express their feelings in acceptable ways.

- They may not have the verbal language to express their feelings.

- They may take the initiative to learn about themselves and their world by testing limits.

- Learning to regulate their behavior and emotions will take time.

- Your job is to use positive guidance to promote children's self-regulation.

Tell participants that they will now have an opportunity to look at some guidance practices to determine whether or not they promote children's self-regulation.

Give each group a copy of handout 4C, "Is This Positive Guidance?" and give these instructions:

- Read each scenario.

- Decide as a group if the scenario is positive guidance.

- Discuss what the teacher did to make it positive guidance or not.

Allow about 10 minutes for group discussions. Then have groups share their decisions with the whole group. Discuss any differences that arise, and clarify the correct answer if necessary.

Trainer's Note: Scenarios 1, 2, and 5 are positive guidance; Scenarios 3, 4, and 6 are not.

Activity 2

Explain that many positive guidance strategies are available for teachers to use to prevent, minimize, and respond to unwanted behaviors. In this activity, participants will look at a wide variety of positive guidance strategies that they can use with infants, toddlers, and twos.

Have participants look back at handout 4C, "Is This Positive Guidance?" Explain that in each positive guidance scenario, the teacher used specific strategies.

Go through each positive guidance scenario and ask participants to name or describe the strategies. Record their responses on chart paper. Add to the responses as necessary.

Possible responses for Scenario 1:

Change the environment; that is, the teacher added the gym knowing that Willard likes to crawl.

Explain the reason; for example, "It's not safe to climb on the stove, you could get hurt."

Show and tell such as when the teacher gently turns the child's body so he can see the gym and explains that he can climb it.

Possible responses for Scenario 2:

Offer an explanation. For example, the teacher says, "Matthew, it is time to go outside. I wish you could stay in but there is no one to stay with you. I can't stay with you because I have other children to care for."

Offer two acceptable choices, such as "Would you rather hold my hand and hop like a bunny to go outside? Or would you rather hold my hand and stomp like an elephant?"

Possible responses for Scenario 5:

Offer encouragement, such as "You're pouring water from the cup to the bowl."

Use "I" statements. For example, the teacher says "When there is water on the floor, I'm afraid someone will slip and fall."

Offer two acceptable choices: "The choice is to keep the water in the water table or to play somewhere else."

Provide an alternative, such as when, after the child and teacher clean up, the teacher takes the child's hand and they walk away together to go play somewhere else.

Distribute handout 4D, "Positive Guidance Strategies." Review the strategies.

Ask participants to look at Scenario 4 in handout 4C. Read the first sentence to the group.

Ask them how the teacher could respond using positive guidance.

Possible responses:

Say, "I see…": "Jonisha, I see that you would like to play with the beads and Melissa is using them right now."

Show and tell: "Jonisha, look at Melissa's face. She is telling you she is upset because you took her beads."

Offer two acceptable choices: "You may ask Melissa for some of her beads or you may get another basket of beads from the shelf."

Model specific language: "Jonisha, say, 'Melissa, may I have some beads please?' Okay, let's practice it together."

Change the environment: If there are not already enough for more than one child to work with, add more beads.

Repeat one of the group's examples using a harsh tone of voice. Then repeat it using a calm tone of voice. Ask the group how the tone of your voice changed the intent of your message. Remind them that how they talk to children is just as important as what they say.

Explain that participants will now have the opportunity to practice responding to children's behaviors using positive guidance strategies.

If participants are not already sitting in groups at tables, have them form small groups of 4–6 people. Distribute a cube, from handout 4E, "Positive Guidance Cube," to each table.

Give the following instructions:

- Take turns rolling the cube.

- Read the scenario that is on top.

- Pick one positive guidance strategy to use to respond to that scenario and describe how to use it. Encourage participants to refer to pages 146–152 in *The Creative Curriculum.*

- Pass the cube to the next person. If someone lands on a scenario that has already been discussed, he or she must offer a different strategy that could be used to respond to that same scenario.

Circulate around the room, offering assistance and support when necessary.

When the groups have finished, read a few of the scenarios and ask volunteers to share some of the techniques that they used.

Summary

Make the following points:

- You now have a wide variety of positive guidance strategies to choose from.

- Practice makes perfect when using new teaching strategies: The more you use them, the more natural they will be for you.

- No single approach works for every child, at every age, and in every situation.

- By practicing the strategies you will learn:

   Which strategies work best under certain circumstances.

   Which strategies work best for the individual children with whom you work.

Guiding Children's Learning: Talking With Infants, Toddlers, and Twos

☐ Baskets

☐ Handout 4F

☐ *The Creative Curriculum,* p. 163

Preparation

Copy handout 4F, "Talking With Infants, Toddlers, and Twos to Guide Their Learning." Cut the handout so that each scenario is on a separate slip of paper. Fold the scenarios and place them in baskets. Make enough so that each table has a basket of assorted scenarios.

Introduction

Make the following points:

- Talking with infants, toddlers, and twos throughout the day is an important strategy for guiding their learning and helping them to make sense of their world.

- Through back-and-forth verbal and nonverbal interactions you have with children every day, you help children build their receptive and expressive language skills and learn to converse.

Activity

Tell participants that in this activity, they will practice using some specific strategies for talking with infants, toddlers, and twos.

Review the following strategies for talking with infants, toddlers, and twos:

- Describe what a child is seeing or doing.

- Verbalize children's emotions.

- Use words to show the value you place on learning and problem solving.

- Express ideas that children will come to understand over time and with experience.

- Provide vocabulary.

- Build their confidence as learners.

- Ask children open-ended questions to extend their thinking.

Distribute one basket of scenarios to each table. Give the following directions:

- Pick one person to begin by selecting a scenario out of the basket.

- He or she should read the scenario, choose a strategy to use to support children's learning, and provide an example of what he or she might say.

- Then, pass the basket to the next person. That person may choose to respond to the last scenario with a new strategy or select a different scenario from the basket.

- Continue practicing until everyone has had at least two turns or until time is up.

Encourage participants to refer to page 163 in *The Creative Curriculum* for help.

Circulate around the room listening and offering feedback and assistance as needed.

When most participants have had enough time to practice, conduct a large-group discussion about the process. Ask:

- What was challenging about this process?

- What was easy for you?

- Were any strategies harder for you to use than others?

Summary

Make the following points:

- Talking with infants, toddlers, and twos is one of the most important ways to guide their learning.

- Through verbal and nonverbal exchanges, you help children make sense of their world, show them that you value their learning, help them express and think about new ideas, encourage them to stretch their thinking and learn new words, and show children that you care about them.

Challenging Behaviors

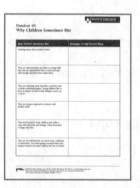

☐ Chart paper
☐ Handout 4G
☐ Handout 4H
☐ *The Creative Curriculum,* pp. 155–158

Preparation

Copy handout 4G, "Temper Tantrums," and handout 4H, "Why Children Sometimes Bite."

Review pages 153–159 in *The Creative Curriculum.*

Introduction

Make the following points:

- Now that you have many positive guidance strategies that you can use in your classrooms, it is time to discuss what to do when a child's behavior is particularly challenging.

- Because these behaviors often stir up strong feelings in people, it is important for you to think about how you will respond before the behavior ever occurs.

Activity

Tell participants that in this activity they will think about two kinds of challenging behaviors that they may frequently encounter in working with toddlers.

Lead participants in the following guided imagery exercise.

- Relax in your chair and, if you feel comfortable, close your eyes. Find a memory of a time when a child's behavior was very difficult for you. Look carefully at your memory. What was the child doing? What were you doing? What were you feeling? What do you think the child was feeling? What are you feeling about it now?

- Let go of these feelings. Gradually come back to the present time, but keep some memories of what these behaviors were and how they made you feel.

- When you are ready, open your eyes.

Explain that everyone who works with young children finds certain behaviors to be particularly difficult or challenging to address. Before talking about addressing specific behaviors, it is important to identify some of the feelings that participants had when they remembered those tough situations.

Ask the group to call out feelings they identified during the guided imagery exercise. List them on chart paper. Point out that these are very strong feelings. Explain that when people feel such strong emotions it can be hard to control how they respond. As teachers, knowing why children engage in very challenging behaviors can help you to make positive guidance choices and stay in control of your emotions.

Remind participants that the first step in responding to challenging behaviors is to try to determine the cause of the behavior. Many possible causes may underlie problem behaviors. For example, children who exhibit these behaviors may not know how to express their feelings in other ways. Infants and toddlers may not have words to use. A child may be tired, teething, or need your attention.

A series of objective, factual observations can lead you to a useful conclusion about a child's behavior. Explain that observation notes must be objective and factual to be useful. Make the following points:

- When your notes include words like *fussy, upset, hyperactive,* or *aggressive,* they reveal your impressions or assumptions rather than what a child actually did or said.

- These judgmental words may or may not tell an accurate story of what actually took place.

When reviewing observation notes look for the answers to these questions:

- What time of day did the behavior occur?

- Who was involved?

- What preceded the unwanted behavior?

As you collect and analyze your observations, you may find a pattern that will help you understand the cause of the behavior.

Teachers who are keen observers can learn to identify the signs that a child may be about to lose control. When they see these signs, they can to step in to guide a child to an activity that reduces the stress and frustration that may result in problem behavior.

Explain that two behaviors are particularly challenging for teachers of toddlers: tantrums and biting.

Make the following points:

- Temper tantrums are no fun for anyone. They leave children feeling exhausted and frightened at their loss of control. They can also leave adults feeling angry, incompetent, and even embarrassed, especially if they occur in public.

- It is important to remember that life can be very frustrating for toddlers. They are struggling with accepting limits that you set for them as well as the limits of their own abilities. They are caught between wanting to be a big kid and sometimes needing still to be a baby.

Give each participant a copy of handout 4G, "Temper Tantrums." Have participants independently complete the first two questions. Then ask them to share their responses with the other people at their table.

Make the following points:

- Once tantrums begin, your first concern should be to keep the child from hurting him- or herself or someone else.

- Reassure the child that you are there until the tantrum is over.

- Show empathy by using active listening. During a tantrum, it is even more important to mirror the feelings with the appropriate tone and facial expressions. "You *really* want that bear. You *want* it, you *want* it, you *want* it."

- Try to stay calm. If your emotions escalate with the child's, it will be harder for the child to calm down.

At their tables, have participants discuss the four proactive strategies listed on page 155 in *The Creative Curriculum*. Ask each table of participants to share its thoughts with the whole group.

Explain that biting, the other specific challenging behavior for mobile infants and toddlers, can be very frightening to both teachers and parents. As with tantrums, focusing energies on prevention is very important.

Distribute handout 4H, "Why Children Sometimes Bite." Explain that the first column of the table describes some of the reasons that children may bite. Instruct participants to work with others at their table to complete the second column of the chart.

Trainer's Note: If there is not enough time for everyone to complete the handout, you may want to instruct half of the group to start at the end of the chart and work back to the beginning.

Debrief as a large group using page 156 in *The Creative Curriculum* as your guide. Make the following points:

- Other behaviors, such as extremely distressed crying, disruptive actions, kicking, hitting, and pushing, can also be challenging when they occur frequently.

- Observing children regularly and recording your observations will allow you to keep track of children's behaviors and recognize patterns.

- Good observations are objective and factual rather than subjective.

Explain that no matter how attentive participants are, it is likely that eventually one child in their program will bite another. It is important to have a procedure in place for what to do when a child bites.

Review pages 157–158 in *The Creative Curriculum* with participants.

Lead a discussion of the following questions with the group:

- When should you seek outside help for a child for challenging behaviors?

  Possible Responses:

  When a teacher feels that she is unable to meet a child's needs on her own.

  If a teacher has tried partnering with the family and using multiple positive guidance strategies and feels that nothing is working.

  If a teacher is concerned that a child may have a developmental delay and thinks the child is in need of screening from an outside agency.

- Who in your organization can help you do that?

Possible Responses

Director

Head Teacher or Lead Teacher

Training and Curriculum Specialist

Family Education Coordinator

Summary

Make the following points:

- Challenging behaviors are often cries for help; children who behave in challenging ways may not know how to express their feelings in other ways.

- Teachers can proactively use a variety of prevention strategies so that challenging behaviors do not occur.

- Careful observation of children helps teachers to identify patterns in problem behaviors.

- Families are your partners and an important source of information when addressing children's challenging behaviors.

- It is important for teachers to know how to make referrals and seek help from outside agencies when they need additional support to help children and families with challenging behaviors.

Notes:

Assessing Children's Development and Learning: An Overview

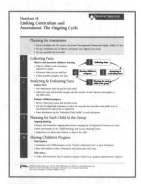

- ☐ 8½" x 11" paper
- ☐ Markers
- ☐ "Family Conference Form"
- ☐ "Individual Child Profile" booklets
- ☐ Handout 4I
- ☐ Handout 4J
- ☐ Handout 4K
- ☐ *The Creative Curriculum,* pp. 47–57, 169–170, 175, and Appendix, p. 424

Preparation

Copy handouts 4I, "Linking Curriculum and Assessment: The Ongoing Cycle," and handout 4J, "Sample Observation Notes."

Trainer's Note: This workshop provides only a brief overview of the assessment system that is an integral part of *The Creative Curriculum.* To use this system well, teachers will need a more in-depth approach on how to write objective observations, analyze them, and use all the forms to plan and share information.

Introduction

Make the following points:

- Assessment is the process of gathering and analyzing information about children in order to make decisions.

- In *The Creative Curriculum,* assessing, caring, teaching, and planning are linked.

Activity 1

Make the following points:

- Assessment means different things to different people.

- It evokes varied feelings in each of us.

Give the following directions:

- Think about the topic of assessment and draw a picture that represents your thinking and feelings.

- Share your drawings with others at your table. Explain to them:

    Why assessment was depicted in this fashion

    What knowledge, skills, or support you need to become more comfortable with the topic

Ask for volunteers to share with the whole group.

Ask: What is the purpose of assessment?

> **Possible answers:**
>
> > *Support learning*
> >
> > *Identification of special needs*
> >
> > *Program evaluation*
> >
> > *Accountability*
> >
> > *Program and school monitoring*

Make the point that we assess children in order to:

- Get to know each child and each child's progress

- Use what we learn to plan for each child and groups of children

- Share information about children's progress

- Improve the program and prepare reports

Explain to participants that you will review the cycle of assessment.

Make the following points:

- Ongoing assessment should be closely tied to curriculum goals and objectives.

- *The Creative Curriculum Developmental Continuum for Infants, Toddlers & Twos* was designed specifically for this purpose.

- Goals and objectives are what you want children to learn.

- A curriculum is your road map for getting there.

- Assessment helps you plan for each child and tells you how the child is progressing on each objective.

- A developmental continuum shows you the steps along the way.

- Using the *Developmental Continuum* will help you observe children in the context of everyday routines and experiences.

- You will be able to assess each child's current level of development and to think about likely next steps. Then you can plan for each child and for groups of children.

- As you learn about each child's strengths, interests, and developmental timetable, use the information and strategies in *The Creative Curriculum* to build responsive relationships and to offer experiences that promote each child's development and learning.

Distribute handout 4I, "Linking Curriculum and Assessment: The Ongoing Cycle." Make the following points:

- Before you begin, you will need to do some planning.

- You need to become familiar with *The Creative Curriculum Developmental Continuum for Infants, Toddlers & Twos.*

- You will set up a system for observing, documenting, and organizing your notes that works for you. Having a system in place for taking and managing observation notes is essential. Your system will keep you organized and save you time.

- To accompany this observation notes system, you will be setting up portfolios for each child that you will use in assessing progress.

Have participants open to pages 169–170 in *The Creative Curriculum* to review ideas for organizing observation notes and portfolio items.

Explain that there are four phases of *The Creative Curriculum for Infants, Toddlers & Twos Developmental Continuum* Assessment System:

- Collecting facts

- Analyzing and evaluating facts

- Planning for each child and for the group

- Sharing children's progress

Notice on handout 4I, "Linking Curriculum and Assessment: The Ongoing Cycle," that we have placed these steps in a circle. It is a cycle that is repeated throughout the year.

The first phase is collecting facts. To collect facts, you document what you see and hear.

- The facts that you collect will answer the question, "What are children doing?"

- To collect facts, you will observe children and document what they are doing by

  - Writing observation notes

  - Collecting portfolio samples

  - Taking photos

  - Making audio or video recordings

  - Getting input from families

The next step in the assessment process is to **analyze the facts.**

- In order to analyze facts, you will ask yourself, "What does this fact mean?" "What does this observation tell me about the child's development and learning?" and "Which goals and objectives does it relate to?"

- Refer to the goals and objectives to decide which objectives apply.

- Record the numbers of the objectives on the note or on the back of the portfolio item.

Have participants open *The Creative Curriculum* to page 175. Review the process of analyzing the observation note on Valisha. Refer participants to the "Goals and Objectives at a Glance," on page 424 of the Appendix in *The Creative Curriculum.*

Distribute the "Individual Child Profile."

Tell participants: Next, you will **evaluate children's progress.**

- You will evaluate children's progress three or four times a year: in the fall, winter, and spring. If you are in a year-round program, you will also evaluate in the summer. We call these points in time Progress Checkpoints.

- To evaluate children's progress, you will make judgments about how children are progressing.

- You will ask yourself, "Which developmental step best describes the child's skills in relation to each objective?"

- To answer this, you will use all the documentation you have collected, your observation notes, the child's portfolio, and information in the *Developmental Continuum.*

- Using the *Developmental Continuum,* you will think about what the child did and said and decide which of the five steps best represents the child's skill level for an objective.

- After making your determination, you will record it on the "Individual Child Profile." This document is used throughout a child's first 3 years.

- If you are in a group setting with co-teachers, you may want to do this together or at least discuss your findings.

The next step is to use what you have learned to **plan for each child and for the group**.

- After you have collected facts, analyzed what they mean, and used the facts to determine progress on the *Developmental Continuum,* what do you do with that information? How do you use that information to guide your planning?

- The *Developmental Continuum* is intended to be used for evaluation purposes and also in an ongoing fashion to plan and individualize for children and to promote progress.

- Teachers engage in a continuous process of observing, reflecting, and responding or planning.

- Two forms are designed for weekly planning, the "Child Planning Form" and the "Group Planning Form."

- The "Child Planning Form" helps you plan for individual children on a weekly basis.

- The "Group Planning Form" enables you to take information about individual children as well as the group and decide on the changes you will make to the environment, materials, schedule, and routines for the week.

Trainer's Note: Responsive planning is discussed in chapter 2, "Creating a Responsive Environment," of *The Creative Curriculum*. An activity on responsive planning that introduces the "Child Planning Form" and the "Group Planning Form" is included in chapter 2 of this Trainer's Guide.

Distribute the copies of the "Family Conference Form."

- The final step in the cycle is to **share with families what you have learned.**

- The "Family Conference Form" is a form for you to use when meeting with each child's family.

- You will write brief statements summarizing their child's progress in each goal area and answering questions about their child.

- Under the appropriate goal heading on the form, highlight a child's new discoveries and the skills he or she has mastered. Offer specific examples from your observation notes.

- This form helps you present examples in the context of curriculum goals, rather than as a random list of children's recent accomplishments. This organization makes the examples more meaningful for the family.

- At conference times, you will share the information with families and seek their input. Together, you will determine the next steps you each will take to support their child's development and learning.

Trainer's Note: Family conferences are discussed in chapter 5, "Building Partnerships With Families," of *The Creative Curriculum*. An activity on conducting family conferences is included in that section of the Trainer's Guide.

Summarize the assessment process by reviewing the handout 4K, "Year at a Glance."

Activity 2

Trainer's Note: If you are able, bring a video clip of a child with you to the training. Show it to participants and ask them to record three observation notes while they watch the video.

Explain to participants that they will have the opportunity to practice the cycle of assessment using an observation of one child.

Distribute handout 4J, "Sample Observation Notes."

Have participants use *The Creative Curriculum* "Goals and Objectives at a Glance" (page 424 of the Appendix) to determine to which objectives the observation relates.

Ask them to select one of the objectives that they chose. Have them open to the page in the *Developmental Continuum* (pages 47–57) that shows the steps for that objective. Direct them to use their observation notes to determine which step best describes the child's level of development for that objective.

Ask volunteers to share the objectives they selected and the step they decided on for their chosen objective.

Next, ask participants to write a plan describing something they could do to support the child's development and learning in relation to the chosen objective and step. Have participants think about the "Child Planning Form" and the "Group Planning Form."

Ask volunteers to share their plans.

Have participants talk with a partner about what information they would record on the "Family Conference Form" to share with families.

Summary

Make the following points:

- Using a systematic assessment system helps you purposefully observe children and document your observations.

- The information you collect enables you to plan experiences that meet each child's needs, interests, and abilities, and to talk with families about their child's development and learning.

Notes:

Building Partnerships With Families

To serve children well, teachers must develop partnerships with families. In a true partnership created to benefit the child, families and caregivers participate equally in the relationship and communicate regularly. By being familiar with the unique characteristics, strengths, and priorities of each family, teachers can find ways to build the trust and respect that are necessary to this partnership.

Purpose

This workshop series explores practical ideas for working with families to develop partnerships based on trust and mutual respect. Participants consider how they can address the special concerns of families with children under the age of 3 and ways that they can get to know families. They examine various strategies for welcoming families, communicating with them, and involving them in their child's program. Finally, participants learn ways to respond to challenging situations by using techniques that support a partnership approach.

Big Ideas

This series of workshops features a number of important ideas, including the following:

- Parents of infants often feel stressed and tired, have conflicting feelings about sharing the care of their child, and want to know everything about their child's day.

- Every family is different. Therefore, teachers need to spend time getting to know each family in order to appreciate the special needs, strengths, and practices that influence their child's development and learning.

- Culture plays an important role in child-rearing practices. Teachers should take time to learn about the cultures of the families in their program so that they can build effective partnerships with them.

- Programs make families feel comfortable by creating a welcoming environment, orienting them to the program, developing an individual care plan for their child, and reaching out to all family members.

- Teachers can communicate with families in a variety of ways, including daily exchanges of information, memos, e-mails, letters, and journals.

- Formal conferences are a time to sit together with a family and have uninterrupted time to share information about the child and plan together.

- When conflicts or differences emerge, teachers need to consider the families' viewpoints as well as their own in order to resolve the problems in ways that support the partnerships and build mutual respect.

- Teachers need to provide special understanding and support to families who are under stress or who are coming to terms with the fact that their child has a disability.

Building Partnerships With Families

Workshops

⚙ WORKSHOP	🔑 KEY POINTS	📄 MATERIALS	🕐 TIME (minutes)
Will My Child Still Love Me Best?: Addressing Families' Concerns (p. 122)	Everything you do to assure families that you and your program will respond positively to their concerns will promote the development of the trust and confidence that are essential to building a partnership.	☐ Chart paper ☐ Markers	30
Getting to Know Families: Appreciating Differences (p. 124)	The more we are aware of our own beliefs and values, the more we can recognize and learn to respect the various beliefs and values of others. Being aware of the challenges that families face can help you respond to them intelligently and empathetically.	☐ Handout 5A. Gaining Self-Awareness	35–45
How Well Do You Know Your Families? (p. 126)	Knowing and appreciating what is unique or different about each family helps teachers build relationships and support children's learning and development.	☐ Handout 5B. How Well Do You Know Your Families? ☐ *The Creative Curriculum*, pp. 185–187	30

⬡ WORKSHOP	🔑 KEY POINTS	📄 MATERIALS	🕐 TIME (minutes)
Communicating With Families (p. 128)	Daily exchanges are the primary way to communicate with family members and keep everyone informed about what is happening at home and in the program. More formal ways of communicating, such as letters, forms, e-mails, and conferences, provide opportunities to share more in-depth information with families.	☐ Family Conference Form ☐ Handout 5C. Individual Care Plan: Family Information Form ☐ *The Creative Curriculum,* pp. 193–201	60
Family Conferences (p. 132)	Formal conferences provide opportunities for teachers and families to strengthen their partnership. Use the conference to share information, observations, and questions, and to solve problems and resolve differences. The "Family Conference Form" can help you plan for and carry out the conference.	☐ Family Conference Form ☐ Handout 5C. Individual Care Plan: Family Information Form ☐ Handout 5D. Preparing for a Family Conference: Role-Play Scenario A ☐ Handout 5E. Preparing for a Family Conference: Role-Play Scenario B ☐ *The Creative Curriculum,* pp. 198–200	60
Building a Partnership With Gena's Family (p. 136)	The parents of a child with a disability are your greatest resource for support and information. Asking questions will let families know that you value their knowledge, insights, and advice about their child.	☐ Chart paper ☐ Markers ☐ Handout 5F. Ivan's Home Visit Notes ☐ *The Creative Curriculum,* pp. 41–43 and 166–167, and chapter 5	60

⚙ WORKSHOP	⚲ KEY POINTS	📄 MATERIALS	⏱ TIME (minutes)
Resolving Differences: A Partnership Approach (p. 140)	Families are vital partners in promoting children's development and learning, and they play an essential role in *The Creative Curriculum*. Recognizing what beliefs and practices influence a family's actions enables you to respond in appropriate and respectful ways.	☐ Handout 5G. Resolving Differences: A Partnership Approach	45
Sharing the Care: Working Through Conflicts With Families (p. 142)	When a family member is clearly upset about a problem, following the steps of conflict resolution will help you resolve the situation positively.	☐ Handout 5H. The Steps of Conflict Resolution ☐ Handout 5I. Conflicts With Families ☐ *The Creative Curriculum*, pp. 209–212	45

Notes:

Will My Child Still Love Me Best?: Addressing Families' Concerns

☐ Chart paper
☐ Markers

Preparation

Write the following questions at the tops of five sheets of chart paper, with one question on each sheet:

- Will my child feel comfortable and happy in this program?

- Will my child still love me best and miss me when we are apart?

- Will my child have interesting things to see and to do?

- Will my child learn to get along with other children?

- Will my child be with adults who know and respect our family?

Hang the five sheets around the room.

Introduction

Make the following points:

- Parents often are uncertain and fearful when they seek care for their infant, toddler, or 2-year-old.

- Everything you do to assure families that you and your program will respond positively to their concerns promotes the growth of the trust and confidence that are essential to building partnerships.

Activity

Explain to participants that in this activity they will think about what it means for new parents to be considering your program for their infant, toddler, or 2-year-old.

Give the following instructions:

- Five questions are written on the charts hanging around the room. Each question is a special concern of families with children under age 3.

- Take a marker with you and circulate around the room.

- On each chart, write something you do in your program to address this concern.

After 15–20 minutes, review the charts with the whole group.

Invite participants to share any personal experiences they've had with putting their own young children in someone else's care.

Summary

Make the following points:

- Thinking about what parents are feeling during this exciting but vulnerable period of their lives helps you to support them as they make the decision to leave their children in your care.

- When you take the time to address families' concerns, you promote the development of the trust and confidence that are essential to building a partnership with each family in your program.

Getting to Know Families: Appreciating Differences

☐ Handout 5A

Preparation

Copy handout 5A, "Gaining Self-Awareness."

Introduction

Make the following points:

- Knowing children means knowing families. Each family differs in its composition, personality, temperament, life experiences, and cultural background and practices.

- When you get to know families and appreciate their differences, you begin building partnerships that support children's learning and development.

- Knowing families enables you to communicate with and involve them in the program in ways that meet their needs and the needs of their children.

- Gaining self-awareness is the place to start.

Activity

Explain to participants that in this activity they will reflect on their own beliefs and values in an effort to gain better self-awareness.

Distribute handout 5A, "Gaining Self-Awareness," and give the following instructions:

- Think about the messages you may have received growing up and the experiences you had in your own family and community.

- Read the questions on handout 5A, "Gaining Self-Awareness," and answer any question to which you have an immediate response.

- Discuss any thoughts you feel comfortable sharing with the person sitting next to you, and talk about how personal experiences might influence a teacher's thinking and actions toward families.

Lead a brief discussion about how personal views can affect our ability to build effective partnerships with families.

Invite participants to share insights they gained from the activity.

Summary

Make the following points:

- The more aware you are of your own beliefs and values, the more you can recognize and learn to respect those that are different.

- Being aware of the challenges that families face can help you respond to them intelligently and empathetically.

- Learn as much as you can about and from the families in your program.

How Well Do You Know Your Families?

☐ Handout 5B

☐ *The Creative Curriculum,* pp. 185–187

Preparation

Copy handout 5B, "How Well Do You Know Your Families?"

Introduction

Make the following points:

- In the same way that you get to know each child and use what you learn to develop a relationship, you begin building partnerships with families by getting to know and appreciate each family.

- Some families are easy for you to get to know, while others require more effort on your part.

Activity

Explain that in this activity participants will assess how well they know the families in their program.

Distribute handout 5B, "How Well Do You Know Your Families?" and give the following instructions:

- For each child in your room, write the family's name in column 1 of handout 5B.

- Reflect on the following questions and discuss your responses with others at your table:

    - Did you remember all of the families' names?

    - Which ones were easier or more difficult to remember? Why?

Have participants open to pages 185–187 in *The Creative Curriculum*. Discuss key points about the differences listed. Give the following instructions:

- In column 2 of handout 5B, write something unique about each family. It may be related to the differences you just discussed or something else.

- Discuss the ways in which you learned about these characteristics.

Emphasize that knowing about each family's unique characteristics and circumstances enables teachers to relate to each family in ways that make them feel valued, respected, and a welcome part of the program.

Ask participants to think about how they might use what they know about a family to build or strengthen a relationship and support children's learning and development. Have them record their ideas in column 3 of handout 5B.

Invite a few people to share some of their ideas.

Summary

Make the following points:

- Knowing children means knowing families.

- Every family is different. Knowing and appreciating what is unique and different about each family helps you build relationships and support children's learning and development.

Communicating With Families

☐ Family Conference Form

☐ Handout 5C

☐ *The Creative Curriculum*, pp. 193–201

Preparation

Review pages 193–201 in *The Creative Curriculum*. Duplicate handout 5C, "Individual Care Plan: Family Information Form," and gather copies of the "Family Conference Form."

Introduction

Make the following points:

- Regular, positive communication helps families stay informed about what their child is learning and what you have learned about their child.

- You communicate with families through informal daily exchanges and through more formal methods, such as conferences. Both are important.

- The "Individual Care Plan: Family Information Form," handout 5C, provides you with specific questions to ask each family. This information will help you learn about the ways in which the families in your program care for their children at home.

- The "Family Conference Form" helps you share information about each child with his or her family, discuss the child's progress, and plan ways of working together to support the child's development and learning.

Activity

Explain that in this activity participants will imagine that their program has been recognized for its excellent communication with families. Because of this, they have been asked by the staff of a nearby program to provide them with ideas that will help them improve their program's communication with families. Assign one of the following topics to a group or groups:

- Making the Most of Daily Exchanges (see pages 195–196 in *The Creative Curriculum*)

- Communicating in More Formal Ways (see page 197)

- Holding Conferences With Families (see pages 198–200)

- Making Home Visits (see pages 200–201)

Ask participants to use the information in *The Creative Curriculum* and from their own experiences working with families to develop the advice they will give to the nearby program.

After 20–30 minutes, invite each group to present their suggestions.

Make or reinforce the following points:

- Daily exchanges are the primary way to communicate with family members and keep everyone informed.

- When communicating with families, be as specific and as factual as possible. Be objective, rather than subjective.

- Some of the more formal ways of communicating are written media, such as newsletters, a daily communication form, and letters to families. It is important to be aware that some families may not be comfortable with written communication because they have limited literacy skills or speak a language other than English. Ask participants to share ideas that they have used successfully in these instances.

- Family conferences are opportunities to share information, observations, and questions, and to solve problems together. Take the time to plan for a family conference.

- Home visits are unique opportunities to see a child and family in their most comfortable setting.

Introduce the "Individual Care Plan: Family Information Form" and the "Family Conference Form." Make the following points:

- Two forms in *The Creative Curriculum* can help you communicate and build partnerships with families.

- The "Individual Care Plan: Family Information Form" is used to develop a plan to care for each child. The questions on the form help you gather information from families about arrival and departure, eating and mealtimes, diapering or toileting needs, and sleeping habits.

- You should complete an "Individual Care Plan: Family Information Form" when a child enters the program and update it whenever patterns change. The form should always be updated during family conferences.

- The "Family Conference Form" is used to summarize a child's progress, record information and ideas from the family, and plan together to support the child's next steps.

Review both forms with the group.

Trainer's Note: See the workshop "Responsive Planning," in chapter 2, "Creating a Responsive Environment," for more information on how to complete the "Individual Care Plan: Family Information Form."

Provide participants with the following information about completing the "Family Conference Form":

- You should complete the first four boxes on the form prior to meeting with families. Use the information you have about each child to write a summary of progress in each goal area. Remember to use observation notes, portfolio items, and information from families to complete those sections. Be sure to do the following:

  - Highlight each child's strengths and interests.

  - Use specific examples rather than vague, sweeping statements.

  - Be positive and respectful in your comments.

- Point out that the remaining sections on the form are completed in partnership with families. Teachers and families both will have something to contribute to these sections:

  - Favorite Activities and Special Interests

  - Situations or Experiences That Cause Distress

  - Next Steps at the Program and at Home

- Teachers should also ask for families' input to complete the section Family Comments and Special Circumstances.

Summary

Make the following points:

- Daily exchanges are the primary way to communicate with family members and keep everyone informed about what is happening at home and in the program.

- Respectful and sincere interactions between families and teachers show children that their home and the program are connected.

- More formal ways of communicating include letters, forms, and e-mails. However, take into account that some families may not be comfortable with written communication.

- Family conferences and home visits provide you with opportunities to share more in-depth information with families. Use the "Individual Care Plan: Family Information Form" and the "Family Conference Form" to do so.

Family Conferences

☐ Family Conference
Form

☐ Handout 5D

☐ Handout 5E

☐ *The Creative Curriculum,* pp. 198–200

Preparation

Review pages 198–200, "Holding Conferences With Families," in *The Creative Curriculum*.

Prepare the handouts, making sure to make enough copies of handout 5D, "Preparing for a Family Conference: Role-Play Scenario A," and handout 5E, "Preparing for a Family Conference: Role-Play Scenario B," to provide each team of partners with a copy

Introduction

Make the following points:

- Formal conferences provide opportunities for teachers and families to strengthen their partnership.

- It is important to prepare for a family conference.

- Use the conference to share information, observations, and questions, and to solve problems and resolve differences.

- Family conferences are usually held four times a year, after completing the "Individual Child Profile" at each checkpoint. The "Family Conference Form" can help you plan for and carry out the conference.

- Update the "Individual Care Plan: Family Information Form" during the conference. On the basis of this information, revise the child's "Individual Care Plan" and your daily schedule as needed.

- After the conference, be sure to follow up on any questions or concerns raised during the conference.

Activity

Have participants look at pages 198–200, "Holding Conferences With Families," in *The Creative Curriculum*. Make the following points:

Before the conference:

- Review your observation notes, the child's portfolio, and the "Child Planning Form."

- Let families know what your intended purpose is for the conference, and find out what the family's goals are for the conference.

- Summarize information from the "Individual Child Profile" to complete the top four boxes (To Learn About Self and Others, To Learn About Moving, To Learn About the World, and To Learn About Communicating) on the "Family Conference Form."

- Be prepared to share specific examples, stories, and observations of the child's experience in your program.

During the conference:

- Use the first conference of the year as a time for you and the family to get to know each other and to start building a partnership. Continue to share developmental information at each subsequent conference, further developing your partnership.

- Set a relaxed tone for the conference by sharing something new, interesting, or delightful that the child has done or said.

- Ask the family open-ended questions so that you can learn from them about their child.

- Ask specific questions so you can update the "Individual Care Plan: Family Information Form."

- Share the "Family Conference Form." Work with the family to complete the four boxes labeled Favorite Activities and Special Interests, Situations or Experiences That Cause Distress, Family Comments and Special Circumstances, and Next Steps at the Program and at Home.

After the conference:

- On the basis of any new information, update the "Individual Care Plan: Family Information Form" and, if necessary, revise the "Individual Care Plan" and your daily schedule.

- Make sure that the family has a copy of the completed "Family Conference Form."

- Address any questions or concerns that the family expressed.

Review the "Individual Care Plan: Family Information Form" and the "Family Conference Form" with the group.

Tell participants that now they will have an opportunity to practice participating in a family conference. Ask everyone to find a partner, preferably someone with whom they have not worked previously, and to decide who will be the teacher and who will be the family member.

Distribute handout 5D, "Preparing for a Family Conference: Role-Play Scenario A." Ask participants to read their role-play information and use that information to complete the handout. Invite participants to invent any additional information they would like to add. Allow participants about 10 minutes to do this.

Invite them to role-play the family conference, using the information from their handout. Allow about 10 minutes for the role-plays. Circulate around the room, offering support and guidance as needed.

Trainer's Note: Many people feel uneasy role-playing in front of a group. This whole-group role-play allows all participants to have a chance to role-play in a comfortable setting, working with a partner, but not in front of a large group.

Ask partners to change roles and distribute Scenario B of handout 5E, "Planning for a Family Conference: Role-Play Scenario B." Allow partners about 20 minutes to complete the handout and role-play the conference in their new roles.

Debrief the activity by asking:

When you were a family member

- How did the teacher make you feel comfortable at the beginning of the conference?

- Did the teacher give specific examples of something new or interesting that your child did? Describe what he or she said.

- What is an example of an open-ended question that the teacher asked?

- How did you feel during the conference?

When you were a teacher

- How did you feel during the conference?

- What is one new thing that you learned about the child?

- What changes would you make to the child's "Individual Care Plan" based on information you learned during this conference?

- What would you do differently next time?

Summary

Make the following points:

- Family conferences are a time to sit down together, uninterrupted; exchange information; and confirm what each of you knows about the child.

- Seek information from the family by asking open-ended questions.

- Complete the appropriate boxes on the "Family Conference Form" together with the family.

- Use the information from the conference to update the "Individual Care Plan" and as the basis for long-term planning for the child.

Building a Partnership With Gena's Family

☐ Chart paper

☐ Markers

☐ Handout 5F

☐ *The Creative Curriculum,*
pp. 41–43 and 166–167,
and chapter 5

Preparation

Copy handout 5F, "Ivan's Home Visit Notes."

Review pages 41–43, 166–167, and chapter 5 of *The Creative Curriculum.*

Introduction

Make the following points:

- Families of children with disabilities will have many of the same concerns as other families but also will want to make sure that you will be able to take care of their child's special needs.

- In addition to using the "Individual Care Plan: Family Information Form," you will have to decide what other information you need for planning routines and experiences that support development and learning for a child with a disability.

Activity

Distribute handout 5F, "Ivan's Home Visit Notes." Read Ivan's notes to the group or have participants read it to themselves.

Give the following instructions:

- You are Ivan's co-teacher in the 2-year-old group.

- As a team, you need to think about what information you will need to make sure Gena is included in all aspects of the program and can successfully participate.

- Divide your chart paper in half.

- Brainstorm what you may need to know to begin planning for Gena. Record all of your questions and concerns on one half of your chart paper.

- Use the information on pages 41–43 and 166–67 in *The Creative Curriculum* for guidance.

After 10–15 minutes, give the following instructions:

- Review your list.

- Now try to determine how you would find answers to these questions:

    - Where would you look for information?

    - Who could you ask to find the answers?

- Refer to pages 41–43 and 166–167 and chapter 5 of *The Creative Curriculum.*

- Record your ideas on the other half of your chart paper.

After 10–15 minutes, invite each group to present their questions and information sources.

Make the following points:

- You may get most of the information you are seeking from talking with the child's family.

- Developing a strong partnership between teachers and the child's family is essential to creating a successful experience for a child with disabilities.

- Asking questions will help you to find out more about the effects of the disability on a particular child.

- Open-ended questions are the most useful in learning about the child and family. These questions typically begin with words such as "why" and "how" or phrases such as "tell me about... ." Open-ended questions encourage a person to describe an idea or give detailed explanations.

With your team, develop at least five thoughtful, open-ended questions you can ask Gena's family to get the information you need.

After 10 minutes, invite each group to present one or two questions.

Summary

Make the following points:

- The parents of a child with a disability are your greatest resource for support and information.

- Asking questions will let families know that you value their insights and advice about their child.

- You will get more information asking open-ended questions rather than questions with a single answer.

Notes:

WORKSHOP

Resolving Differences: A Partnership Approach

☐ Handout 5G

Preparation

Copy handout 5G, "Resolving Differences: A Partnership Approach."

Introduction

Make the following points:

- In spite of your efforts to build positive partnerships with families, misunderstandings will occur.

- Sometimes a family's wishes or values may conflict with your own.

- By learning as much as possible about each family and understanding beliefs and practices that may differ from yours, you gain insights into the causes of misunderstandings.

- These insights can help you resolve differences in ways that build trust and respect.

Activity

Explain that in this activity participants will practice working through differences with families.

Distribute handout 5G, "Resolving Differences: A Partnership Approach."

Read the situation in the first row, inviting ideas on ways to handle the situation that promote a partnership.

> **Possible responses:**
>
> *Acknowledge the parents' concerns and perspective.*
>
> *Suggest that all of you observe the child closely for the next few weeks and then meet again.*
>
> *Offer to have someone from the program accompany the family.*
>
> *Arrange to have a specialist observe the child in the program.*

Have each group read the remaining examples and discuss how they might handle those situations in positive ways. Give these instructions:

- Examine the situation from the perspectives of the teacher and of the family.

- Generate an approach that expresses a partnership view.

- Record your ideas in the column titled "A Partnership View."

After most are finished, invite participants to share their responses with the whole group.

Summary

Make the following points:

- Every family is different and is worthy of respect.

- Families are vital partners in promoting children's development and learning and play an essential role in *The Creative Curriculum.*

- Recognizing what beliefs and practices are behind a family's actions enables teachers to respond in respectful ways.

Sharing the Care: Working Through Conflicts With Families

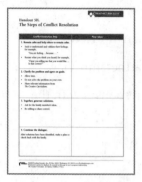

☐ Handout 5H

☐ Handout 5I

☐ *The Creative Curriculum,* pp. 209–212

Preparation

Copy handouts 5H, "The Steps of Conflict Resolution," and 5I, "Conflicts With Families."

Cut apart the scenarios on the copies of handout 5I, so that each group of participants will get one scenario.

Introduction

Make the following points:

- If you do not try to resolve an issue that is bothering you or a family member, you will probably become annoyed or frustrated. Avoiding an issue rarely solves the problem and sometimes makes it worse.

- Knowing the steps to follow to resolve the conflict can help lead you to a positive resolution.

- Because conversations about a conflict can sometimes be emotional, they are better handled away from the children and other families.

- If you are working with children when an upset family member approaches you, suggest delaying the conversation until you can find someone to take over. Then you can give the family member your full attention in a more private place.

Activity

Have participants turn to pages 209–212 in *The Creative Curriculum*. Review the steps of conflict resolution with the participants. Have a volunteer read text from the "What a Parent Says" column in the charts while you read from the "How You Respond" column.

Explain to participants that they will now have the opportunity to practice working through conflicts with families.

Have participants form small groups of 3–4 people. Distribute handout 5H, "The Steps of Conflict Resolution." Distribute one scenario from handout 5I, "Conflicts With Families," to each group.

Give these instructions:

- Read the information in the scenario about what the family member is thinking and what he or she says.

- After reviewing pages 209–212 in *The Creative Curriculum*, consider the steps of conflict resolution and how you would use them to work through this conflict with the family member.

- Think of questions you could ask to encourage the family member to share more of his or her thoughts.

- Record your ideas on handout 5H.

After most groups are finished, read each scenario and invite groups to share their responses with the whole group.

Summary

Make the following points:

- When a family member is clearly upset about a problem, you want to respond in ways that lead to a positive resolution. It is helpful to know what steps to follow to resolve the conflict.

- Remain calm and help others to remain calm by seeking to understand the family member's position and validating their feelings.

- Work with the family to clarify the problem and agree on shared goals for their child.

- Together, generate solutions that let families know that you are partners in caring for their child.

- Keep communicating with the family, agreeing on a time to talk about whether or not the solutions are working or what changes need to be made.

Workshops on Routines

Routines are opportunities to build relationships with children that promote the development of trust. The one-on-one time teachers spend easing a child and family through hellos and good-byes, diapering and toileting, feeding, dressing, and soothing a child to sleep helps infants, toddlers, and twos learn to trust and feel secure. As children gain new skills and can participate more actively in daily routines, they develop a sense of their own competence. Routines are also times to nurture children's curiosity and guide them as they make increasing sense of their world.

Purpose

These workshops examine the five routines that are discussed in *The Creative Curriculum*. Participants explore the importance of each routine and how they can support children's development and learning through specific caring and teaching practices. They learn strategies for creating an environment that supports the five routines. Finally, participants consider the importance of partnering with families to make routines into rich learning opportunities for children.

Big Ideas

Among the important ideas to be learned in the series of workshops on routines are the following:

- A child's stage of development influences how he or she handles hellos and good-byes. Because these times of the day involve strong feelings, teachers and families need to work together to help children cope with these transitions and feel in control.

- Diapering is a time to focus attention on one child, play games, talk, and build a relationship. As children gain the control needed to begin using the toilet, teachers need to work closely with families to help children achieve this important milestone.

- Mealtimes and related activities, such as setting the table, washing hands, talking with others, and brushing teeth, are all learning opportunities. During mealtimes, children can explore the tastes, colors, textures, and aromas of foods and experience a sense of caring and community.

- Knowing how each child falls asleep and awakens can help you manage sleeping and nap time with a group of infants, toddlers, and twos in ways that allow all children to get the sleep they need.

- Getting children dressed and undressed are one-on-one times to build a relationship with each child and encourage children to participate increasingly in the process as they gain new skills.

Introduction to Routines

Workshops

⚙ WORKSHOP	⚲ KEY POINTS	📄 MATERIALS	🕐 TIME (minutes)
The Routine of Routines (p. 148)	Consistent and nurturing routines meet the physical and social/emotional needs of children, help them build trust and autonomy, encourage secure attachments, and support children's development and learning.	☐ Chart paper ☐ Markers in five different colors ☐ Basket ☐ Handout IR–1. Routines: Discussion Cards ☐ Handout IR–2. Action Plan for Routines ☐ *The Creative Curriculum,* pp. 1–17 and chapters 6–10	60
Your Own Views (p. 152)	As you implement *The Creative Curriculum* in your program, you may need to adapt your personal beliefs and values to fit curriculum guidelines.	☐ Handout IR–3. Your Own Views: Discussion Cards	30
Sharing the Value of Routines With Families (p. 154)	Working with families to provide consistency between home and your program is essential to helping children have good experiences during routines.	☐ Markers ☐ Chart paper ☐ *The Creative Curriculum*, chapters 6–10	50
Responding to What Children Need (p. 156)	Observing children carefully during routines can help you support their development as you respond appropriately to their individual needs.	☐ Handout IR–4. Responding to What Children Need ☐ *The Creative Curriculum*, p. 284 and Appendix, p. 424, "Goals and Objectives at a Glance"	45

The Routine of Routines

- [ ] Chart paper
- [ ] Markers
- [ ] Basket
- [ ] Handout IR–1
- [ ] Handout IR–2
- [ ] *The Creative Curriculum,* pp. 1–17 and chapters 6–10

Preparation

Copy handout IR–1, "Routines: Discussion Cards." Make the number of copies needed to provide each participant with one card. Cut apart the discussion cards, fold them, and put them in a basket.

Make one copy of handout IR–2, "Action Plan for Routines," for each participant.

Introduction

Ask participants to call out the first words that come to mind when they think of routines. Record their responses on chart paper.

Compare the responses to a dictionary definition of *routine*:

> "A prescribed course of action to be followed regularly, a standard procedure. A set of customary and often mechanically performed procedures or activities."[1]

Discuss the idea that infants, toddlers, and twos experience routines somewhat differently from the way adults do. Make the following points:

- Responding consistently to children is necessary to being able to meet the physical and social/emotional needs identified by Abraham Maslow, T. Berry Brazelton, and Stanley Greenspan.

- The positive ways teachers handle routines with young children helps children build trust and autonomy, as explained by Erik Erikson.

- Children develop secure attachments to the adults who implement routines in consistent, nurturing, and caring ways.

- Because routines are such a major part of daily life, they should be as manageable, consistent, nurturing, and supportive as possible.

[1] Pickett, J. (Ed.). (2000). *The American heritage dictionary of the English language* (4th ed.). Boston: Houghton Mifflin Company.

Activity

Explain that, in this activity, participants will discuss ways that teachers can prepare for routines so that they are nurturing, go smoothly, and support children's learning.

Form five groups by having participants draw a routine card from the basket. Participants with the same routine discussion card form a group.

Give each group a different colored marker and a few pieces of chart paper.

Explain the following:

- Write the name of your routine at the top of the chart and select a recorder.

- Brainstorm all of the things you can do to make this daily routine go smoothly.

- Identify specific practices you can use during the routine to make it a nurturing experience.

- Identify ways that you can support children's development and learning during the routine.

- Look back at pages 1–17 in *The Creative Curriculum* and note which theory and research supports your routine.

- You will have 3 minutes at each chart. When the 3 minutes are up, you will move on to the next chart and repeat the task.

Give a 15-second warning before the 3-minute period is over. At the end of the 3 minutes, ask each group to move, with their markers, to the next chart.

Allow a minute for them to read what is already on the chart and then begin the next 3-minute period. Using their own markers, each group should add any new ideas they have about the topic.

After every group has contributed to all of the charts and has moved back to their original starting place, have them review the ideas on their chart. Tell participants to find the chapter in *The Creative Curriculum* that relates to their routine. Have them look through the chapter and add any new ideas to their charts.

When finished, ask all the groups to post their charts around the room.

Distribute handout IR–2, "Action Plan for Routines."

Have each group present its chart to the rest of the participants.

Encourage participants to fill in the handout as they hear new ideas that they would like to try in their own programs.

After all the groups have presented, engage participants in a large group discussion. Ask:

- What were the common themes you heard as you listened to each other's presentations about routines?

- Would anyone like to share an idea she or he is especially eager to try?

Have participants open to page 219 in *The Creative Curriculum*. Review the organization of the routine chapters.

Summary

Make the following points:

- Routines are important parts of the day for infants, toddlers, and twos.

- Because they are so important, routines should be as manageable, consistent, nurturing, and supportive as possible.

- Consistent and nurturing routines meet the physical and social/emotional needs of children, help them build trust and autonomy, encourage secure attachments, and support children's development and learning.

Notes:

WORKSHOP

Your Own Views

☐ Handout IR–3

Preparation

Copy handout IR–3, "Your Own Views: Discussion Cards," and cut the cards apart. Sort them into piles so that all copies of the four cards related to the same routine are in one pile.

Introduction

Make the following points:

- Some of your attitudes and personal beliefs may support what you are learning about good early childhood practices; others may conflict with what you are learning.

- As you implement *The Creative Curriculum*, take time to consider how your opinions, experiences, and beliefs affect your view of each particular routine and how *The Creative Curriculum* aligns—or does not align—with your values and beliefs.

Activity

Divide participants into five groups. Have each group choose one person to be the facilitator and one person to be the recorder. Give each group facilitator one set of the question cards.

Provide the following instructions:

- The facilitator will read each question on the card.

- As a group, discuss your responses to the questions. Please answer as honestly as you feel comfortable doing.

- The recorder will take notes on the discussion to share with the group. The recorder should not include individuals' names.

After participants have completed their discussions, have each group share their questions and highlights from their discussion. Encourage participants in other groups to offer their thoughts on questions as well.

Trainer's Note: After the training, you may want to make notes about the responses so that you can use this information to plan future trainings. Also consider using the discussion cards for a particular routine as a way to introduce a workshop for that routine.

Summary

Make the following points:

- As you implement *The Creative Curriculum* in your program, you may need to adapt your personal beliefs and values to fit curriculum guidelines.

- Keep your own views in mind as you continue to learn about *The Creative Curriculum* so you know what specific adaptations you will have to make to follow good early childhood practices.

WORKSHOP

Sharing the Value of Routines With Families

☐ Markers
☐ Chart Paper
☐ *The Creative Curriculum,* chapters 6–10

Preparation

Review the letters to families ("Sharing Thoughts About …") about each routine on pages 231, 245, 261, 275, and 287 in *The Creative Curriculum.*

Introduction

Make the following points:

- Working with families to provide consistency between their homes and your program is essential to helping children have good experiences during routines.

- It is important to explain to families the importance of routines so that, together, you can make routines rich learning opportunities for children.

Activity

Explain that in this activity, participants will have the opportunity to share information with families about the routines in *The Creative Curriculum.*

Instruct participants to pick a routine that interests them.

Give the following instructions:

- Your group is responsible for communicating with families about your chosen routine.

- First, brainstorm the following on chart paper:

  - What is important about your routine for an infant, toddler, or 2-year-old?

  - What questions or concerns might families have about your routine?

  - How can you work in partnership with families to increase consistency between home and your program?

- You may want to refer to the chapter in *The Creative Curriculum* that relates to your routine.

After about 10 minutes, give the following directions:

- Now that you have identified the information that is important to communicate to families about your routine, work together to decide how you would share this information with families that are new to your program.

When the groups are finished, have them share their charts and ideas with the group.

Summary

Make the following points:

- Partnerships with families enable you to provide consistent care for each child.

- Letters to families can invite them to be your partners in making routines rich learning opportunities for children.

Responding to What Children Need

☐ Handout IR–4

☐ *The Creative Curriculum*, p. 284 and Appendix, p. 424

Preparation

Copy handout IR–4, "Responding to What Children Need."

Introduction

Observing children carefully during routines can help you support their development as you respond appropriately to their individual needs.

Activity

Explain that, in this activity, participants will have the opportunity to reflect on a child's behavior during a routine and to respond appropriately.

Have participants turn to page 284 in *The Creative Curriculum*. Read the scenario and review the teacher's thoughts and questions, her response, and what Abby might be learning.

Distribute handout IR–4, "Responding to What Children Need."

Instruct participants to turn to the appendix of *The Creative Curriculum*, p. 424, "Goals and Objectives at a Glance."

Have participants work with a partner to complete handout IR–4.

When all groups are finished, discuss participant responses.

Summary

Make the following points:

- Observing children during routines allows you to make thoughtful decisions about how best to meet their needs.

- Daily routines provide opportunities for children to develop and learn.

Notes:

Hellos and Good-Byes

Workshops

⚙ WORKSHOP	🔑 KEY POINTS	📄 MATERIALS	🕐 TIME (minutes)
Saying Good-Bye Is Hard To Do (p. 160)	Separating and reuniting with loved ones is a lifelong process that brings out strong feelings in adults as well as in the infants, toddlers, and twos in your program.	☐ Handout 6A. Saying Good-Bye Is Hard to Do: Children's Responses to Good-Byes ☐ *The Creative Curriculum,* pp. 225–226	40
Reunions (p. 162)	Reunions at the end of the day can be just as emotional for children and families as good-byes in the morning.	☐ Handout 6B. Reunions Can Be Hard, Too! ☐ *The Creative Curriculum,* p. 230	40
Good or Bad Practice (p. 164)	Hellos and good-byes offer opportunities to build positive, trusting relationships with children and families	☐ Handout 6C. Hellos and Good-Byes: Practice Cards ☐ *The Creative Curriculum,* pp. 223–227	35

WORKSHOP

Saying Good-Bye Is Hard To Do

☐ Handout 6A

☐ *The Creative Curriculum*, pp. 225–226

Preparation

Prepare handout 6A, "Saying Good-Bye Is Hard to Do," and cut the scenarios into strips. Fold the strips and put them in a basket. Prepare enough baskets of scenarios so that each table gets one complete set.

Introduction

Make the following point:

- Separating and reuniting with loved ones is a lifelong process that brings out strong feelings in the adults as well as children in our programs.

Activity

Invite participants to get comfortable in their chairs, take a few deep breaths, clear their minds, and prepare to participate in a guided-imagery exercise.

Guide participants through the following:

> *Close your eyes and imagine you are at the airport. All around you, people are greeting loved ones or saying good-bye. You are standing next to the most important person in your life. You realize that, in a few moments, he or she will board a waiting airplane that will take the person far away—for how long, you don't know. It's time to say good-bye. How do you feel?*

Allow time for participants to think through the scenario. Then ask for volunteers to share their imagined responses.

Ask:

- Would you have felt better if I had said, "It's okay, he'll be back soon," or "You have all of us to keep you company so you won't miss her at all," or "Why don't we go to the movies so you don't think about him?"

Sometimes, this is how adults respond to children's distress during hellos and good-byes. We disregard their feelings or try to distract them from their feelings.

Have participants discuss with the people at their table the strategies they use to help children and families manage hellos and good-byes.

Ask participants to share some of their ideas with the large group. Have them review pages 225–226 in *The Creative Curriculum*.

Tell participants that they will now have the opportunity to practice responding to children during drop-off time.

Give one basket of scenarios to each table. Give the following instructions:

- Take turns choosing a scenario from the basket and reading it to the group.

- Share how you would respond to the child in the scenario to support him or her during hellos and good-byes.

After about 15 minutes, invite groups to share some of their scenarios and responses.

Summary

Make the following point:

- Disregarding or distracting a child from his feelings offers an upset child little support and does not help him build a trusting relationship with you.

- Observing young children and empathizing with their distress and joy will help you to respond appropriately to each child during hellos and good-byes.

Reunions

☐ Handout 6B
☐ *The Creative Curriculum*, p. 230

Preparation

For each group, make a copy of handout 6B, "Reunions Can Be Hard, Too!"

Introduction

Make the following points:

- Reunions at the end of the day can be just as emotional for children and families as good-byes can be in the morning.

- A child who said good-bye easily or who adjusted well after a painful good-bye may greet her father joyfully or ignore him. She might also have a temper tantrum or begin to cry, because she saved her strong feelings for her family, the people she trusts most. The happy response delights her father, but the others might make him feel rejected, sad, or guilty.

- Departures need your attention as much as arrivals.

Activity

Have participants form groups of three and give them the following instructions:

- With the people in your group, role-play your scenario. One of you will be Mercedes, one will be Matthew, and one will be Matthew's dad.

- After you role-play the scenario, complete handout 6B, "Reunions Can Be Hard, Too!"

- Each of you should respond to the sections on the handout that relate to your part. For example, if you were Matthew's father in the scenario, tell the others what you were thinking and feeling when Matthew ignored you and said, "No!"

- Next, decide how Mercedes should respond to support Matthew and his father. Think about how Matthew and his dad might react to the response.

- In relation to your chosen response, look at the goals and objectives and decide what Matthew might be learning.

After about 15 minutes, invite groups to share their responses and to discuss what Matthew might be learning from each response.

Have participants open to page 230 in *The Creative Curriculum* and read the recommended response.

Summary

Make the following points:

- Reunions can be just as challenging for children as arrivals can be. They can elicit strong feelings in both children and their families.

- By being responsive to each child's needs and offering caring explanations to families, you can help children and families reunite at the end of the day.

Good or Bad Practice

☐ Handout 6C

☐ *The Creative Curriculum,* pp. 223–227

Preparation

Prepare handout 6C, "Hellos and Good-Byes: Practice Cards." Make enough copies to provide each group with a complete set, and cut apart the cards.

Introduction

Make the following points:

- Children, their families, and you all experience strong feelings during hellos and good-byes.

- Hellos and good-byes offer opportunities to build positive, trusting relationships with children and families.

Activity

Explain that in this activity, participants will look at a variety of practices related to hellos and good-byes.

Have participants form groups of 4–6 people. Give each group a set of cards.

Provide the following instructions:

- Each card describes a practice that teachers could use during hellos and good-byes.

- With the people at your table, read each practice and sort them into two piles: good practices and bad practices.

- Using the five blank cards, record five additional good practices that you use in your room to support hellos and good-byes.

After all groups have finished sorting the practices and adding their five, have them check their answers by reviewing pages 223–227 in *The Creative Curriculum.*

Ask each group to create a top-10 list of their favorite practices from the good-practices pile. They may include any of their additional five. Explain that they should also select one bad practice and explain why they think it is not a good practice to follow.

Have each group present their top-10 good practices. Also have each group describe the bad practice they selected and explain why it is a bad practice.

Seven bad practices were on the cards given to participants:

1. Encourage parents to sneak out if their child is very distressed at drop-off time.

2. Encourage a child to join the group as soon as possible, even if he is very upset.

3. Encourage families to be quick about saying good-bye. Long good-byes only make it harder for the child to separate.

4. Establish a policy of dropping off children outside of the room so the child learns to separate more quickly from her family.

5. Do not approach a child or family member until a child has stopped crying.

6. Make sure you do not give a crying child a lot of attention after his family member leaves. This will only encourage more crying in the future.

7. Two-year-olds should be able to say good-bye to their families easily. Remind them that big boys and girls don't cry when their mommy or daddy leaves.

Summary

Make the following points:

- Learning to separate is a lifelong process and an important part of growing up.

- When you help children learn to manage separations from and reunions with their loved ones, they feel understood and gain self-confidence.

Diapering and Toileting

Workshops

⚙ WORKSHOP	🔑 KEY POINTS	📄 MATERIALS	🕐 TIME (minutes)
A Time for Caring and Teaching (p. 168)	Taking your time and interacting with children during diapering will help children feel good about themselves and learn about their bodily functions.	☐ Large baby doll ☐ Diapering supplies ☐ Chart paper ☐ Markers ☐ *The Creative Curriculum*, p. 240	30
Supporting Toilet Learning (p. 170)	Two-year-olds are about to accomplish a special task—toilet learning—and you have an important role to play. Partnering with families will make toilet learning a more positive experience for each child.	☐ Chart paper ☐ Markers ☐ Handout 7A. Supporting Toilet Learning ☐ *The Creative Curriculum*, pp. 242–245	25
Looking at the Goals and Objectives (p. 172)	Diapering and toileting both offer many opportunities for you to support children's development and learning.	☐ *The Creative Curriculum*, p. 234 and Appendix, p. 424, "Goals and Objectives at a Glance"	40

A Time for Caring and Teaching

- [ ] Large baby doll
- [ ] Diapering supplies
- [ ] Chart paper
- [ ] Markers
- [ ] *The Creative Curriculum*, p. 240

Preparation

Review pages 237–240 in *The Creative Curriculum*.

Label the chart paper "Keys to a Great Diaper Change."

Introduction

Make the following points:

- Sometimes teachers find themselves racing through diaper changes or wishing that all the children they care for had already graduated to underpants.

- When this happens, it is important to remind yourself that diapering and toileting are times for caring and teaching. What you say and do make a difference in what children learn and how they feel about themselves.

Activity

Explain to the group that you are going to change a baby's diaper.

Perform a quick, efficient diaper change. Do not talk to the baby or smile while you do it.

Trainer's Note: If this is your program, or if you are familiar with the diaper-changing steps of the program where you are training, follow the program's procedure. If not, tell the group not to focus on the steps you use.

Have participants open to page 240 in *The Creative Curriculum* and read the scenario with Brooks and Abby.

Tell participants that they need to help you improve the way you change diapers. Have them direct you in your second attempt to give the child a good learning and development experience during the diaper change.

Ask: What made the second experience better?

Record their responses on the chart paper you earlier labeled "Keys to a Great Diaper Change."

Possible responses:

Took your time

Told the child what was happening

Asked the child questions

Talked about bodily functions

Labeled items of clothing and body parts

Smiled

Ask:

- How do you think the baby felt about the first diaper change?

- How did she feel about the second?

Summary

Make the following points:

- Each child's diaper is changed several times a day. These times are opportunities for you to give special, individualized attention to each child.

- Taking your time and interacting with children during this routine will help children feel good about themselves and learn about their bodily functions.

WORKSHOP

Supporting Toilet Learning

☐ Chart paper

☐ Markers

☐ Handout 7A

☐ *The Creative Curriculum,* pp. 242–245

Preparation

Review pages 242–245 in *The Creative Curriculum*.

Duplicate handout 7A, "Supporting Toilet Learning."

Introduction

Make the following points:

- Two-year-olds are about to accomplish a special task— toilet learning—and you have an important role to play.

- Partnering with families will make toilet learning a more positive experience for each child.

Activity

Have participants form groups of 4–6 members. Ask each group to choose one person to be the group recorder. Give the following instructions:

- With the people in your group, discuss the questions on handout 7A, "Supporting Toilet Learning."

- Record your responses on the chart paper.

After about 15 minutes, instruct participants to review pages 242–245 in *The Creative Curriculum*. Encourage them to add any new ideas from the book to their group's list of ideas.

After the groups have finished, have them share those of their ideas that were not in the book.

Summary

Make the following points:

- Knowing the signs of toilet-learning readiness will help you and families transition children to using the toilet when they are ready.

- Talking with children about using the toilet, frequently reminding children to go to the toilet, and acknowledging children's successes are important ways to support toilet learning.

- Talking with families about toilet learning is essential to helping children have positive experiences while learning this new skill.

WORKSHOP

Looking at the Goals and Objectives

☐ *The Creative Curriculum*, p. 234 and Appendix, p. 424

Preparation

Review chapter 7, "Diapering and Toileting" (pp. 232–245), of *The Creative Curriculum*.

Introduction

Make the following points:

- If a child's diaper is changed six times a day until he is 30 months old, he will have had his diaper changed more than 5,400 times. Anything experienced 5,400 times is an important part of life for the child who experiences it and for those who create the experience.

- Diapering offers you a chance to focus all of your attention on a single child.

- Two-year-olds are learning to accomplish a very important task—toilet learning—and you have an important role to play.

- Diapering and toileting both offer many opportunities for you to support children's development and learning.

Activity

Explain that in this activity participants will think about what happens during diapering and toileting and how they can use this routine to support children's development and learning.

Have participants form four groups and open *The Creative Curriculum* to the appendix, page 424, "Goals and Objectives at a Glance."

Assign one goal to each of the four groups.

Give the following instructions:

- For each objective in your goal area, think of what you can observe children doing during diapering and toileting that relates to the objective.

- Next, think of something that you could do or say to support children's development and learning related to each objective.

- If your group has the goal "To learn about moving," please come up with several examples for each of your two objectives.

- Use page 234 in *The Creative Curriculum* as a reference.

Give the groups 15–20 minutes to complete their discussions.

Have each small group share their ideas with the large group. Pose these questions:

- Which objectives were easy to link to observations and practices?

- Which were more difficult to link?

Summary

Make the following points:

- Diapering and toileting are times for teachers to interact individually with children.

- These routines offer many opportunities for you to support children's social/emotional, physical, cognitive, and language development and learning.

Eating and Mealtimes

Workshops

⬡ WORKSHOP	🔑 KEY POINTS	📄 MATERIALS	🕐 TIME (minutes)
Creating a Safe, Healthy Environment for Eating and Mealtimes (p. 176)	Eating and mealtimes and related activities, like all routines, are opportunities for learning and nurturing experiences. It's also important to pay attention to health and safety issues during these routines.	☐ Handout 8A. Eating and Mealtimes: Is This Good Advice?	60
Eating With Infant Hands (p. 178)	When going through routines with infants, toddlers, and twos, it is important to remember what you know about child development so that you can best support children's growing abilities.	☐ Masking tape ☐ Paper towels ☐ O-shaped cereal ☐ Paper cups ☐ Water	60
Feeding Infants and Toddlers (p. 180)	During mealtimes, you can build a positive relationships with children as you nurture their bodies.	☐ Bananas ☐ Saltine crackers or teething crackers ☐ Handwashing wipes ☐ Handout 8B. Introducing New Foods: A Toddler Adventure ☐ *The Creative Curriculum,* pp. 251–253 and 255–259	60

Creating a Safe, Healthy Environment for Eating and Mealtimes

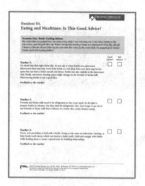

☐ Handout 8A

Preparation

Review pages 249–255 in *The Creative Curriculum*.

Copy handout 8A, "Eating and Mealtimes: Is This Good Advice?" on card stock. Make enough copies so that each group of participants has one of the scenarios and its five pieces of advice.

Introduction

Make the following points:

- Like all routines, mealtimes and related activities—such as setting the table, washing hands, talking with others at the table, and brushing teeth—are learning opportunities.

- However, in addition to making sure that this routine is a nurturing experience for infants, toddlers, and twos, it's very important to pay attention to safety and health practices.

- You need to know general guidelines for health and safety practices during mealtimes, such as those recommended by the American Academy of Pediatrics. You also need to know your state and local regulations concerning food handling and your own program's policies and procedures.

- It's important to set up an environment for eating and mealtimes that supports good health and safety practices.

Activity

Tell participants that in this activity they are going to focus on setting up the environment and health and safety practices as they relate to eating and mealtimes.

Divide participants into groups of six and give each group one scenario with its five advice cards. Allow about 5 minutes for each group to read its scenario and advice and to prepare to present it to the group. Instruct them to assign roles so that, while one person reads the scenario, the others are each one of the advisers.

Trainer's Note: If you are working with a small group or have a limited amount of time for this activity, you might want to delete one of the advice cards for each group. Be sure, however, to include the content of the omitted advice cards when you debrief the activity.

Invite each group to present its scenario and advice. Have the other participants decide whether each piece of advice is good or bad. Encourage participants to share additional information about the topic.

Summary

Make the following points:

- There is a lot to know about setting up the environment and health and safety practices for eating and mealtimes.

- It is important to take time to get good information about health and safety practices, to get trained on health and safety procedures, and to practice specific procedures such as handwashing until you can do them automatically.

- To get good advice, consult information from the American Academy of Pediatrics, check state and local regulations, and review your program's practices.

Eating With Infant Hands

- ☐ Masking tape
- ☐ Paper towels
- ☐ O-shaped cereal
- ☐ Paper cups
- ☐ Water

Preparation

Review pages 255–258 in *The Creative Curriculum*.

Prepare one container of O-shaped cereal for each table.

Introduction

Make the following points:

- Infants and toddlers are developing the fine-motor skills they need to learn how to feed themselves. Before developing a pincer grasp, an infant must use her whole hand to pick up food.

- As they acquire skills and become more independent, they can participate more in self-feeding. They are learning personal care skills as well as feeling confident and competent.

- During mealtimes, young children are also learning about the world. As they eat different foods, they explore the textures, smells, and tastes. They also may be exploring cause and effect.

Activity

Explain that, in this activity, participants will have the opportunity to eat a snack while pretending that they have infant hands.

Have one volunteer from each table be responsible for serving the snack to the rest of the people at the table.

Ask the servers to take enough paper towels and cups for their group, a small container of O-shaped cereal, and a pitcher of water, and then to serve each participant at their table.

Give each table a couple of rolls of masking tape.

Have participants loosely wrap masking tape around their dominant hand to keep the tip of the thumb from touching the other fingertips. Participants should wrap the tape across their knuckles, around the first joint of their thumb, and across their palm, continuing until the band is complete. To pick up small objects, the entire hand will have to be used.

When all participants have prepared their "infant hands," invite them to try to eat their cereal. Ask them to be attentive to the ways they handle the food. Next, encourage them to take a drink of water.

When everyone has experimented with the cereal and the water, ask participants to describe what they noticed about eating and drinking with infant hands.

Summary

Make the following points:

- When going through routines with infants, toddlers, and twos, it is important to remember what you know about child development so that you can best support children's growing abilities.

- Children's bodies typically develop from the core to the extremities. This helps to explain why a pincer grasp is only possible after much experience with a whole-hand grasping technique.

- Although it can be messy, encouraging children to feed themselves contributes to their fine-motor development and builds self-confidence.

WORKSHOP

Feeding Infants and Toddlers

- ☐ Bananas
- ☐ Saltine crackers or teething crackers
- ☐ Handwashing wipes
- ☐ Handout 8B
- ☐ *The Creative Curriculum*, pp. 251–253 and 255–259

Preparation

Review pages 251–253 and 255–259 in *The Creative Curriculum*.

Cut bananas in quarters.

Make copies of handout 8B, "Introducing New Foods: A Toddler Adventure."

Introduction

Make the following points:

- During eating and mealtimes, you build a positive relationship with each child while you nurture their bodies.

- For infants, who need to be fed on demand, bottle-feeding is an important one-on-one experience with you.

- While toddlers and twos may begin to eat in small groups on a more regular schedule, mealtimes should still be relaxed, nurturing experiences.

Activity

Ask participants to find a partner. If possible, request that they work with someone they don't know well or have not already worked with in the workshop.

Distribute the handwashing wipes to each person and one fourth of a banana to each pair.

Tell participants to decide who will be the teacher in this activity and who will be an infant. Instruct the teacher to feed the banana to the infant. There are two rules: No self-feeding, and the child has to finish eating the banana piece.

Debrief the activity by asking the following questions:

- How did it feel to be fed?

- How did you react as an infant to the two rules (no self-feeding and eating the entire piece)?

Distribute the two saltine crackers or one teething cracker to each pair. Ask participants to switch roles. This time there are no rules, and the teacher's goal is to make the interaction as positive and nurturing as possible for the infant. Have each small group share their ideas with the large group.

Pose these questions:

- How did it feel to be fed?

- How did the teacher make the experience comfortable?

- What things did you, as an infant, want to control?

- What can teachers do to make mealtimes relaxed and pleasant?

- What can teachers do during mealtimes to introduce new words and concepts?

Trainer's Note: It's also fun to do this activity with unfamiliar food. For example, some participants may not be familiar with sugared ginger or tomatillos. If you use unfamiliar food, ask participants to share their reactions to being fed an unfamiliar food. Make the point that an infant is having this experience every time a new food is introduced.

Refer participants to pages 251–253 and 255–259 in *The Creative Curriculum* for additional ideas.

Distribute handout 8B, "Introducing New Foods: A Toddler Adventure." Instruct participants to read the initial scenario, which describes how three toddler teachers handled introducing a new food to their toddler groups. Tell them that they will read three responses; decide whether each response is appropriate or inappropriate; and, in the feedback section, explain their decision. Then they will do the same with the second scenario.

Allow about 10 minutes for the activity. Then ask participants to share their decisions and discuss the feedback that they provided.

Summary

Make the following points:

- How you handle the routine of eating and mealtimes can help you build trust with children and support their developing autonomy.

- Being with you is an important part of children's mealtime experience.

- Infants are more comfortable when they are fed by their primary teacher as much as possible.

- Toddlers and twos like to sit and eat with their primary teacher, but they also enjoy meals with other children.

- Good experiences at mealtimes help children develop positive attitudes toward food and nutrition.

Notes:

Sleeping and Nap Time

Workshops

⚙ WORKSHOP	🔑 KEY POINTS	🗎 MATERIALS	⏱ TIME (minutes)
Sleep-Time Routines (p. 186)	Strengthening your relationship with each child, knowing how each child falls asleep and awakens, and partnering with families can help this routine go smoothly.	☐ Chart paper ☐ Markers ☐ Handout 9A. Sleeping and Nap Time: Your Own Views ☐ *The Creative Curriculum*, pp. 268–270 and Appendix, pp. 425–427, "Individual Care Plan: Family Information Form"	30
Sing a Sleep-Time Song (p. 188)	Music and movement can be used to enhance the routine of sleeping and nap time.	☐ Chart paper ☐ Markers	30
Sleep-Time Books (p. 192)	The experience of enjoying stories and books can enhance the routine of sleeping and nap time.	☐ Variety of children's sleep-time books ☐ Handout 9B. A Sleep-Time Book for Children ☐ Handout 9C. Recommended Books for Sleeping and Nap Time ☐ Handout 9D. Annotated Bibliography of Sleep-Time Books for Infants, Toddlers, and Twos ☐ *The Creative Curriculum*, Appendix, p. 424, "Goals and Objectives at a Glance"	45

Sleep-Time Routines

☐ Chart paper
☐ Markers
☐ Handout 9A
☐ *The Creative Curriculum*, pp. 268–270 and Appendix, pp. 425–427

Preparation

Review pages 263–275 in *The Creative Curriculum*.

Copy handout 9A, "Sleeping and Nap Time: Your Own Views."

Introduction

Give these instructions:

- Take a few minutes to think about how you fall asleep at night.

- What bedtime routines help you relax?

- Share your routines with the people at your table and come up with a list of bedtime routines to present to the rest of the group.

As each group presents their bedtime routines, write their ideas on chart paper. Point out that, like adults, individual children have different needs. Ask:

- How do you find out what each child needs?

- How do you accommodate the different needs of the children in your group?

Discuss the groups' responses and make the following points:

- From birth, children differ in how much sleep they need, how soundly they sleep, the regularity of their sleep patterns, and the length of time they need to fall asleep and wake up.

- Strengthening your relationship with each child and knowing how each child falls asleep and awakens can help you manage nap time with your group.

- Working in partnership with families will help you to promote consistency for children between sleeping at home and at your program. The "Individual Care Plan: Family Information Form" (see *The Creative Curriculum* appendix, pages 425–427) can help you gather information from families.

Activity

Distribute handout 9A, "Sleeping and Nap Time: Your Own Views." Assign each group one of the questions to discuss.

Invite each group to share important points from their discussion.

Have participants review the suggestions for caring and teaching during sleeping and nap times on pages 268–270 in *The Creative Curriculum*. Invite comments and questions.

Have participants review the questions related to sleeping and nap time on the "Individual Care Plan: Family Information Form." Conduct a brief discussion with participants, asking the following questions:

- How would you use the information on the form in your program?

- How often would you update the information?

Summary

Make the following points:

- Knowing the specific needs and preferences of each infant, toddler, or 2-year-old in your group will make sleeping and nap times go more smoothly.

- Set up your environment to create peaceful places for children to sleep.

- Talk with families about how they help their children fall asleep, and follow family practices when possible. The information on the "Individual Care Plan: Family Information Form" can help you individualize care for children and promote consistency between their homes and your program.

WORKSHOP

Sing a Sleep-Time Song

☐ Chart paper
☐ Markers

Preparation

Review chapter 9, "Sleeping and Nap Time" (pages 263–275), and chapter 14, "Connecting With Music and Movement" (pages 343–355), in *The Creative Curriculum*.

Write the words to the example lullaby (in the Activity section below) on chart paper, a transparency, or a PowerPoint slide.

Introduction

Make the following points:

- Throughout the world, family members croon lullabies to soothe children to sleep.

- You can use many familiar lullabies to sing children to sleep. You probably have some favorite lullabies, perhaps those that your family sang to you or songs that you sing to your own children.

- Listening to a lullaby can help a fretful child fall asleep. Playing a lullaby at sleep time and nap time in a child care program can help create a calm, peaceful environment that, in turn, can help a child wind down and transition from being active and awake to being relaxed and asleep. When you sing a lullaby to a child to help her fall asleep, you show that you care about her well-being and security.

- At sleep time and nap time, lullabies are a wonderful way to provide consistency between children's homes and the program. In *The Creative Curriculum*, experiences and routines often go together. In this workshop, we will look at how the music and movement can enhance the routine of sleeping and nap time.

Activity

Distribute a piece of chart paper to each group and give the following instructions:

- In this activity, you will make up a simple, easy-to-sing lullaby to share with the whole group.

- Listen to my example. (Sing the following words to the tune of "London Bridge" or make up your own to share.)

  Now it's time for you to rest, you to rest, you to rest.

  It's what you do the very best, all night long.

- Select the melody of a familiar children's song.

- Make up new words to the song. Remember to keep the words simple and to make the song easy to sing.

- Think about how to introduce and use your song with the infants, toddlers, or twos in your group.

- Create at least one variation. For instance, change the words or add motions.

Allow each group about 10 minutes to create a song and a variation.

Invite each group to share its song and variation with the whole group. After each group presents, invite participants to think of other variations to the song.

Ask participants to share the titles of their favorite lullabies.

Trainer's Note: You may want to invite participants to write the words of their favorite lullaby on a piece of paper. You can make copies and distribute them as a resource.

Summary

Make the following points:

- Singing lullabies to children is a way to link *The Creative Curriculum* experience of music and movement to the routine of sleeping and nap time.

- You can choose among many familiar lullabies to sing.

- Lullabies can help create a calm atmosphere for sleeping and help lull children to sleep.

- Families can share the lullabies that they sing to their children at home. Singing them in your program strengthens the link to children's families, languages, and cultures.

- You can create special lullabies to sing to the children in your group.

Notes:

WORKSHOP

Sleep-Time Books

- ☐ Children's sleep-time books
- ☐ Handout 9B
- ☐ Handout 9C
- ☐ Handout 9D
- ☐ *The Creative Curriculum*, Appendix, p. 424

Preparation

Review chapter 9, "Sleeping and Nap Time" (pages 263–275), and chapter 13, "Enjoying Stories and Books" (pages 323–341), of *The Creative Curriculum*.

Copy the three handouts: handout 9B, "A Sleep-Time Book for Children"; handout 9C, "Recommended Books for Sleeping and Nap Time"; and handout 9D, "Annotated Bibliography of Sleep-Time Books for Infants, Toddlers, and Twos."

Collect high-quality children's books that are related to sleeping and nap time. Your collection may include story books as well as concept books that help children learn sleep-time skills. See handout 9C, "Recommended Books for Sleeping and Nap Time," for a list of suggested books, or create a list of your own. You also could ask participants to bring in one of their favorite sleep-time books. Be sure to have at least one book that is suitable for reading with a small group.

Introduction

Make the following points:

- Many families and teachers tell bedtime stories or read to children as part of their sleep-time rituals.

- There are many beloved children's books, such as *Goodnight Moon*, that children want to hear read again and again as they drift off to sleep. Other books, such as *Quiet Loud*, help children learn concepts that are related to sleeping and nap time.

- You can learn a lot about the development of infants, toddlers, and twos by how they respond when you are reading a sleep-time book.

- In this workshop, we will look at how the experience of enjoying stories and books can be used to enhance the routine of sleeping and nap time.

Activity

Explain that, in this activity, participants will have an opportunity to review a sleep-time book and answer questions about how they would use it with young children.

Assign each group a children's book to review. Distribute handout 9B, "A Sleep-Time Book for Children," and give the following instructions:

- Read the children's book that has been assigned to your group.

- As a group, answer the questions on handout 9B, "A Sleep-Time Book for Children."

Read the questions with the participants before they begin. Give the following example for the last question:

> *As you read* Goodnight Moon *to a young infant, she might snuggle into your lap and lean her head against your chest. This behavior is related to Objective 1, "Trusts known, caring adults," in the* Developmental Continuum.

Allow about 15 minutes for each group to read the book and answer the questions.

Invite each group to share its responses with the whole group. Ask for volunteers to read their books aloud.

Place the children's sleep-time books at various tables around the room. Distribute handout 9D, "Annotated Bibliography of Sleep-Time Books for Infants, Toddlers, and Twos." Review the description of *Goodnight Moon* in the first row. Invite participants to walk around the room, look at the books, and write a description of several books on handout 9D. Encourage them to add their own favorites to the list.

Trainer's Note: You or the participants can collect the annotated lists and distribute them to teachers and families.

Summary

Make the following points:

- When you read a sleep-time book to an infant, toddler, or two, you are introducing children to the joys of storytelling and to the sounds and rhythms of language.

- Some sleep-time books teach children concepts and vocabulary that relate to sleeping and nap time. You can read these books to children throughout the day, individually or in a very small group.

- You can learn about children's development by observing them while you are reading a sleep-time book.

- Favorite sleep-time books can help build a bridge between families and the program.

Notes:

Getting Dressed

Workshops

⚙ WORKSHOP	🔑 KEY POINTS	📄 MATERIALS	🕐 TIME (minutes)
How Getting Dressed Supports Development and Learning (p. 198)	Like all routines, getting dressed helps infants, toddlers, and twos develop their social/emotional, physical, cognitive, and communication skills.	☐ Small sticky notes ☐ Handout 10A. How Getting Dressed Supports Development and Learning ☐ *The Creative Curriculum,* Appendix, p. 424, "Goals and Objectives at a Glance"	30
Responding to What Children Need (p. 200)	While dressing may seem like the most ordinary of daily routines, it offers many opportunities to interact and build a child's sense of competence.	☐ Long-sleeved sweaters with buttons ☐ *The Creative Curriculum,* pp. 279–282	45
Working in Partnership With Families (p. 204)	Sharing ideas can help you and families both have successful dressing experiences with their children.	☐ Handout 10B. Sharing Thoughts About Getting Dressed ☐ *The Creative Curriculum,* pp. 280 and 287 and Appendix, pp. 425–427, "Individual Care Plan: Family Information Form"	60

WORKSHOP

How Getting Dressed Supports Development and Learning

- [ ] Small sticky notes
- [ ] Handout 10A
- [ ] *The Creative Curriculum*, Appendix, p. 424

Preparation

Review chapter 10, "Getting Dressed" (pages 277–287), of *The Creative Curriculum*.

Copy handout 10A, "How Getting Dressed Supports Development and Learning."

Introduction

Make the following points:

- Like all routines, the routine of getting dressed helps infants, toddlers, and twos develop their social/emotional, physical, cognitive, and communication skills.

- Children also build language and literacy skills, discover mathematical relationships, and explore like scientists during consistent caregiving routines. For example, while getting dressed or during diapering and toileting, children begin to learn about groups as they learn about things that go on their head or feet. They also learn about order as they see that socks go on before shoes.

- It is important to take time with dressing and to approach this routine as a learning opportunity.

Activity

Instruct participants to work in groups of three or four. Have them brainstorm all of the skills they used this morning when they got dressed, writing each skill on a different sticky note. Allow about 3 minutes to complete this activity.

Distribute handout 10A, "How Getting Dressed Supports Development and Learning," and give the following instructions:

- Using the handout, sort your sticky notes into the four goals of *The Creative Curriculum*.

- When you have sorted them all, notice whether most of the skills relate to one goal. (For example, participants may have identified many fine-motor skills such as zipping, buttoning, tying, or buckling.)

- Talk about which of the skills are appropriate for their children and at what age.

- Are there any goals for which you have not listed skills? Can you think of an appropriate skill for that goal?

Refer participants to the "Goals and Objectives at a Glance" chart on page 424 in the appendix of *The Creative Curriculum*. Ask them to identify specific objectives related to the skills they noted above.

Summary

Make the following points:

- Getting dressed helps infants, toddlers, and twos learn about themselves and others, about moving, about the world, and about communicating.

- You can support children in developing and learning these skills when you approach getting dressed as a learning opportunity.

Responding to What Children Need

☐ Large, long-sleeved sweaters with buttons

☐ *The Creative Curriculum,* pp. 279–282

Preparation

Review pages 279–282 in *The Creative Curriculum.*

Collect several long-sleeved sweaters with buttons (or plan to use participants' sweaters).

Introduction

Make the following points:

- Although dressing may seem like the most ordinary of daily routines, if you take time to pay attention to each child during dressing times, you will find many opportunities to interact with the child and to build his or her sense of competence.

- *The Creative Curriculum* includes practical suggestions about making dressing routines work well for you and the children.

Activity 1

Tell participants that in this next activity they will look at the time involved in getting dressed.

Ask for a pair of volunteers for each large sweater you have collected. Also ask for a volunteer with a watch that has a second hand to be the timekeeper for the activity. Have each pair decide who will be the teacher and who will be a toddler. Give each teacher a sweater. Tell the teachers that, at the signal, they should put the sweater on the toddler and fasten at least three buttons, as quickly as possible without hurting their partner. Note the time that it took to get the toddler dressed.

Ask volunteer partners to repeat the demonstration, keeping the same roles. At the signal, have teachers once again put the sweater on the child. However, this time, tell them to take time to make the routine comfortable for the child, to encourage the toddler to participate in getting dressed, and to make getting dressed into a learning opportunity. Note the time that it took to get the toddler dressed this time.

Ask the participants who played toddlers to discuss the differences in their rushed and leisurely experiences. Ask both partners to explain what the teacher did the second time to make the routine more enjoyable.

Possible responses:

Made eye contact

Asked for cooperation

Described the parts of the routine to the toddler

Have the timekeeper compare the times of the two dressing experiences. Emphasize that very little additional time was needed to make the routine more enjoyable.

Activity 2

Explain that in the next activity everyone will become an expert on one aspect of caring for and teaching children during dressing.

Have participants count off from 1 to 8, to form eight groups. Assign each group a suggestion from *The Creative Curriculum* for making dressing work well, as follows:

- Group 1: page 279, last paragraph ("Supply dress-up clothing …")

- Group 2: page 280, last paragraph ("Handle children's bodies with respect.")

- Group 3: page 281, first paragraph ("Talk with children about what you are doing.")

- Group 4: page 281, second paragraph ("Be aware that children's temperaments …")

- Group 5: page 281, third paragraph ("Let children participate …")

- Group 6: page 282, second paragraph ("Give children choices …")

- Group 7: page 282, third paragraph ("Engage children with songs, …")

- Group 8: page 282, last paragraph ("Step in to minimize frustration …")

Tell participants to read their section and be prepared to share the information with the other people in the group.

Allow about 2 minutes for participants to read their section.

Tell participants that they will now mingle and share the information about their section with participants who read a different section.

Ask for a volunteer and demonstrate a quick exchange of information with the volunteer.

Tell participants to circulate around the room, sharing with different partners until they have received information about most of the other selections. Remind them that it's okay to talk to more than one person from a particular group because they are likely to get different information from each.

Allow about 15 minutes for participants to circulate and then ask participants to take their seats.

Ask for comments or questions.

Conduct a brief discussion about the following questions from "Your Own Views" (page 280) in chapter 10, "Getting Dressed," of *The Creative Curriculum:*

- How do you feel when a child protests about getting dressed?

- How do you help minimize protests and make getting dressed as easy and enjoyable as possible for both you and the child?

Summary

Make the following points:

- The dressing routine is rich in learning possibilities and is an opportunity to focus on one child at a time.

- You can use many strategies to make this routine work well.

- The more they are able to take time with routines, the more teachers and children can enjoy the time together.

- To be successful, routines such as dressing must be done *with* children, rather than *to* children.

Notes:

WORKSHOP

Working in Partnership With Families

☐ Handout 10B

☐ *The Creative Curriculum*, pp. 280, 287, and Appendix, pp. 425–427

Preparation

Review pages 286–287 in *The Creative Curriculum*.

Copy handout 10B, "Sharing Thoughts About Getting Dressed."

Introduction

Make the following points:

• Families may experience some of the same joys and struggles you have while dressing their child.

• Sharing ideas can help you and families both have successful dressing experiences.

• The "Individual Care Plan: Family Information Form" (in *The Creative Curriculum*, appendix, pages 425–427) includes space to record information that families share about dressing.

Activity

Distribute handout 10B, "Sharing Thoughts About Getting Dressed."

Ask participants to read the introduction to the letter.

Then instruct them to work in pairs (or small groups) to complete the letter with 3–5 ideas about how programs and families can work together on the routine of getting dressed. Allow about 10 minutes for the activity.

Invite participants to share some ideas with the whole group.

Ask them to compare their answers with the "How We Can Work Together" section of "Sharing Thoughts About Getting Dressed," on page 287 in *The Creative Curriculum*.

Refer to the "Individual Care Plan: Family Information Form" (in *The Creative Curriculum*, appendix, pages 425–427) and review the question in the dressing section. Ask participants what kinds of information they may receive from families in response to this question.

Conduct a discussion about the following questions from the "Your Own Views" section (page 280) of chapter 10, "Getting Dressed." Ask:

- Do you make suggestions to families about what their children should wear to your program?

- How do you feel when families do not follow your suggestions?

- Can you think of some reasons why they do not follow your advice?

Summary

Make the following points:

- Work in partnership with families to share ideas for a successful dressing experience with their child.

- The "Individual Care Plan: Family Information Form" and the letter to families, "Sharing Thoughts About Getting Dressed," can help build this partnership.

Trainer's Note: The activity of writing a letter to families and comparing it with the corresponding one in the book can be used with any of the routines and experiences in *The Creative Curriculum.* It can also be part of an overview workshop on either routines or experiences.

Workshops on Experiences

Teachers plan meaningful experiences by selecting materials that match children's growing abilities and interests, by observing what children do, and by reflecting on those observations. Knowing how to engage children in a variety of experiences enables teachers to provide them with a rich array of potential learning opportunities. It is important to remember that teachers are only planning for possibilities because they must respond to momentary changes in children's strengths, needs, and interests as well as to their general abilities.

Purpose

This workshop series explores the eight types of experiences that are discussed in *The Creative Curriculum*. Participants learn strategies to support children's development and learning by caring and teaching during play experiences. Participants consider ways to create an environment for each type of experience and explore ideas for sharing their knowledge about the experiences with families.

Big Ideas

The series of workshops on experiences presents many important ideas, including the following:

- Any object that young children can explore can become a toy in a child's hands. Effective toys capture children's attention, keep them engaged, and help them acquire and strengthen new skills.

- Imitation and pretend play are among the most important ways that young children learn about the world and relationships with people.

- By reading books and sharing their pleasure in language and stories, teachers offer important experiences. Children develop a foundation for literacy when they explore books and hear stories read aloud every day.

- Music and movement can be joyful experiences for young children, beginning at birth. When you rock babies to a gentle lullaby, sing a favorite song over and over, or dance around the room with children, you share special moments.

- Art for infants, toddlers, and twos is a sensory experience. They enjoy making marks on paper, tearing paper, and moving fingers through slippery finger paint.

- Young children enjoy food preparation activities when they are allowed to squish, mash, stir, smear, scrub, beat, and knead and then enjoy tasting what they helped to make.

- Sand and water offer wonderful sensory experiences and are calming materials that keep children happily engaged. The addition of a few simple props can extend children's play.

- The outdoors offers an entirely different environment for children to explore and enjoy. Children should go outdoors every day to settings that are designed for their growing abilities and interests.

Introduction to Experiences

Workshops

⚙ WORKSHOP	🔑 KEY POINTS	📋 MATERIALS	🕐 TIME (minutes)
Introducing the Experiences (p. 210)	Eight types of experiences are presented in *The Creative Curriculum*. Each experience chapter gives guidance on how to support children's development and learning, how to create an environment and select materials for the experience, and how to care for and teach children during these experiences. Each chapter ends with a letter to families.	☐ Chart paper ☐ Markers ☐ Tape ☐ Sticky notes ☐ *The Creative Curriculum*, p. 290	60
Responding to Children During Experiences (p. 216)	As you observe young children during experiences, it is important to think about the goals and objectives of the *Developmental Continuum*. Consider what each child is learning and how you might respond.	☐ Child Planning Form ☐ Group Planning Form ☐ Handout IE–1. Observe, Reflect, and Respond ☐ *The Creative Curriculum*, Appendix, p. 424, "Goals and Objectives at a Glance"	45
Sharing the Value of Experiences With Families (p. 218)	It is important to appreciate the value of each type of experience and how it supports children's development and learning so that you can explain your program to families.	☐ Props related to each experience ☐ Paper ☐ Chart paper ☐ Markers ☐ *The Creative Curriculum*, chapters 11–18	70-90

Introducing the Experiences

☐ Chart paper
☐ Markers
☐ Tape
☐ Sticky notes
☐ *The Creative Curriculum*, p. 290

Preparation

Post eight pieces of chart paper on the walls around the room. Label each with one of the experiences.

Introduction

Explain to participants that chapters 11–18 of *The Creative Curriculum* offer guidance about providing appropriate materials and interactions for engaging children in the following eight experiences:

1. Playing with toys

2. Imitating and pretending

3. Enjoying stories and books

4. Connecting with music and movement

5. Creating with art

6. Tasting and preparing food

7. Exploring sand and water

8. Going outdoors

Activity

Give the following instructions:

- Think about what the children in your group did yesterday as they played.

- Using the sticky notes on your table, record brief descriptions of what your children did. Use one sticky note for each situation. For example, you might write "played with the shape sorter" on one note and "looked at board books" on another.

- Record at least 10 different play situations.

After about 5 minutes, explain to participants that they are now going to sort their descriptions of what their children did yesterday by placing their sticky notes on the related experience charts hanging around the room. If participants think a situation is an example of more than one type of experience, encourage them to write it on multiple sticky notes and post them on the related charts.

After all the sticky notes have been sorted, review the charts with the participants. Notice which experience has the most sticky notes and which has the fewest. Ask participants why they think this happened. Ask participants for any examples of play situations that belonged in more than one category.

As you review each experience chart, give the following brief overviews of each experience, in addition to reading a few of the participants' examples.

Playing with toys

- There is an enormous variety of toys for infants, toddlers, and 2-year olds.

- Some of the best toys for young children are common objects and natural materials, such as large plastic bottle tops, cardboard boxes, crinkly tissue paper, wooden utensils, and safe objects you can find outdoors.

- Any object that young children can explore, put together, take apart, push or pull, stack, or bang becomes a toy in a child's hands.

- Effective toys capture children's attention, keep them engaged, and help them acquire and strengthen new skills.

Imitating and pretending

- Pretending is a way of learning as well as a way of playing, and it requires a great deal of thinking.

- Young infants imitate facial expressions, language sounds, and the actions of the people with them.

- Toddlers and twos remember past experiences and often purposefully pretend to be something or someone else, such as a great big scary monster or a daddy feeding a baby.

- Children learn about managing their feelings as they act out emotions in a safe environment. They use imitation to make sense of their experiences and to interact with others socially.

Enjoying stories and books

- Sharing stories and books with young children can be among the most treasured times of your day.

- With so many excellent books to touch, look at, and listen to, children will grow to love books.

- Your interactions as you snuggle together with a book, your enthusiasm, the way you bring a story to life through your dramatic reading, and your interesting questions make the experience special for very young children.

Connecting with music and movement

- Most people enjoy listening to, creating, and moving to music. Music affects our emotions and inspires movement.

- Just as young children want to hear their favorite stories again, they like to hear and sing their favorite songs repeatedly. They also love to make music by hitting a pot with a spoon or by playing real instruments.

- As infants, toddlers, and twos move to music in different ways, they stretch their bodies and their imaginations. Whether they move their hands in fingerplays or move their whole bodies as they dance, children respond to the rhythm and beat of music and the related words.

Creating with art

- Art for infants, toddlers, and twos is largely a sensory experience. By providing a variety of art experiences for young children, they discover that certain materials feel interesting and are fun to use.

- Through art experiences, children learn that they can control and make marks with a variety of tools and materials. Older twos begin to understand that the pictures, models, and constructions they make can represent people and things.

- Young children are interested in what different materials are like and what they can do with them. They are not intent on making a product. Painting lines on paper with a brush and tearing paper into pieces are satisfying experiences by themselves.

Tasting and preparing food

- When you invite children to taste and otherwise explore a new food or include them in helping you prepare a snack, you are promoting more than good nutrition. Food and related conversation and activities encourage development and learning in all areas.

- Tasting and preparing food are part of everyday living with infants, toddlers, and twos.

- At first, children are primarily interested in squishing, mashing, and smearing food. Before long, they become eager and able to help prepare some of the foods they eat, especially because they like to participate in activities that are important to adults.

- Whether it is scrubbing a carrot or dipping a slice of apple in melted cheese, children enjoy and are proud to help you with meaningful tasks.

Exploring sand and water

- Sand and water should be readily available and provide wonderful sensory experiences. They are soothing materials that can calm children and keep them happily engaged.

- Being held by someone they love and the effects they get by kicking and slapping the water are satisfying experiences. Providing cups, rubber toys, pails, and scoops encourages mobile infants to extend their play.

- Sand and water play are usually among the favorite activities of toddlers and twos, who purposefully explore, experiment, and pretend with tools and other objects.

Going outdoors

- The outdoors offers an entirely different environment for children to explore. Outside, children experience fresh air and weather, and the outdoor environment offers more open space in which they can stretch and run.

- Infants, toddlers, and twos should go outdoors every day unless the weather is extreme or the air quality poses a health risk. All young children need natural spaces that encourage sensory, physical, and social exploration.

- When they are outdoors, children can explore the natural world, interact with others, practice gross motor skills, garden, ride trikes, and go on neighborhood walks.

Have participants open to page 290 in *The Creative Curriculum*. Review the organization of the experience chapters.

Summary

Make the following points:

- *The Creative Curriculum* offers guidance for eight types of experiences.

- Each chapter explains how the experience supports children's development and learning, how to create an environment and select materials for the experience, and how to care for and teach children during the experiences. The chapter ends with a letter to families that explains the experience.

Notes:

Responding to Children During Experiences

☐ Child Planning Form
☐ Group Planning Form
☐ Handout IE–1
☐ *The Creative Curriculum,* Appendix, p. 424

Preparation

Copy handout IE–1, "Observe, Reflect, and Respond."

Introduction

Make the following points:

- As you observe children while they are participating in experiences, think about the goals, objectives, and steps of *The Creative Curriculum® Developmental Continuum for Infants, Toddlers & Twos.*

- Take time to appreciate what each child is learning and how you might respond.

Activity

Explain that, in this activity, participants will practice the process of thinking about and responding to children during play.

Distribute handout IE–1, "Observe, Reflect, and Respond." Review the example together. Have participants work with a partner to complete the rest of the chart.

Have participants open *The Creative Curriculum* to the appendix, page 424, "Goals and Objectives at a Glance."

When the participants are done, review the chart with the group, asking volunteers to read their reflections and responses.

Distribute the "Child Planning Form" and the "Group Planning Form." Encourage the participants to talk with a partner and answer these questions:

- What could teachers plan for different experiences based on the observation, reflection, and response?

- What would you add to the "Child Planning Form" for one of the children in the handout?

- What would you add to the "Group Planning Form" on the basis of this information?

Summary

Make the following points:

- As you observe young children during experiences, think about the goals and objectives of the *Developmental Continuum*. Consider what each child is learning and how you might respond.

- In developing weekly plans, use your observations and refer to the *Developmental Continuum* to plan for each child and the group.

WORKSHOP

Sharing the Value of Experiences With Families

☐ Props related to each experience

☐ Paper

☐ Chart paper

☐ Markers

☐ *The Creative Curriculum*, chapters 11–18

Preparation

Collect a variety of props that relate to each of the eight types of experiences.

Make a table sign for each of the experiences.

Introduction

Make the following points:

- Families may not always see the value in every experience you offer to the children in your room.

- It is important to understand why each experience is important and how it supports children's development and learning so that you can explain your program to families.

Activity

Explain that in this activity, participants will practice talking with families about the value of experiences.

Instruct participants to choose one of the eight experiences and to sit at the appropriate table. If an experience is not selected, ask for volunteers to switch groups so that there are at least two people at each table. If there are not at least 16 participants, exclude some of the experiences.

Give the following instructions:

- You must include the following in your presentation:

  - An overview of the experience

  - How your room environment supports the experience

  - How you guide children's learning during the experience

  - An overview of what children learn through the experience

  - A sample of something you might plan for the children related to the experience

- In your presentation, you may use chart paper, markers, and any of the props that are at your table.

Give participants 25–30 minutes to create their presentations. Have each small group present their experience to the rest of the participants. While one group is presenting, encourage the other participants to ask questions about the experience being presented.

Summary

Make the following points:

- Every experience in *The Creative Curriculum* supports children's development and learning.

- Your room should be designed so that there are places and times for children to participate in all of the experiences.

- It is important to understand why each experience is important and how it supports children's development and learning so that you can explain your program to families.

Playing With Toys

Workshops

⚙ WORKSHOP	🔑 KEY POINTS	📄 MATERIALS	⏱ TIME (minutes)
Designing an Ideal Toy (p. 222)	An ideal toy is age appropriate and safe. It captures children's attention, keeps them engaged, and helps them gain and strengthen new skills.	☐ A collection of "beautiful junk" ☐ Supplies such as string and masking tape ☐ *The Creative Curriculum,* pp. 291–300	60
Talking With Children As They Play With Toys (p. 224)	Young children find a responsive adult more fascinating than almost any toy. Your involvement in a child's play makes the experience even more meaningful and enjoyable.	☐ "Child Planning Form" ☐ Handout 11A. Talking With Children as They Play With Toys ☐ *The Creative Curriculum,* pp. 302–304	45

Designing an Ideal Toy

☐ Beautiful junk

☐ Supplies such as string and tape

☐ *The Creative Curriculum*, pp. 291–300

Preparation

Review pages 291–301 in *The Creative Curriculum*.

Provide a variety of beautiful junk that participants can use to make a toy. These items could include cardboard, large plastic bottle caps, egg cartons, clean plastic containers and bottles, fabric scraps, plastic ice cube trays, juice lids, plastic scoops (e.g., from coffee cans), oatmeal boxes, paper towel tubes, ribbons, plastic hangers, empty boxes of all sizes, wooden or plastic spools, safe objects from outdoors, corks, wooden and plastic cooking utensils, and tissue paper.

Introduction

Ask participants to think back to when they were very young children.

- What was your favorite toy?

- What did you do with it?

- Why did you like it?

Make the following points:

- Some of the very best playthings for infants, toddlers, and twos are not commercial toys. They are common objects and natural materials that children can explore safely.

- An ideal toy is appropriate for a child's age and capabilities, can be used safely, captures children's attention, keeps them engaged, and helps them gain and strengthen new skills.

Activity

Give the following instructions:

- You are the early childhood specialist on the design team for a toy company. The team has been charged with designing an ideal toy for a particular age-group.

- At your table, select the age-group for your toy: young infants (birth to 9 months), mobile infants (8–18 months), toddlers (16–25 months), or twos (24–36 months).

- On pages 294–298 in *The Creative Curriculum*, review the toy suggestions for the age-group you have selected, and discuss what makes them appropriate.

- Take whatever beautiful junk appeals to you and design an ideal toy for your age-group, keeping in mind that it has to be safe for children to use (refer to page 293 for safety guidelines) and it must promote children's development and learning (see page 292 for additional information).

- Consider how you would adapt or use the toy with a child who has a disability (see pages 299–300 for ideas).

Allow enough time for each group to create their toy. Then give these instructions:

- The design team now turns into a marketing team. Your task is to plan a marketing campaign that will convince parents that they should buy this toy for their child because it will promote learning and development.

- See page 292 for some ideas to get you started.

Invite each team to give a marketing presentation on their toy to the full group. Remind them that marketers have to both educate and persuade.

Summary

Make the following points:

- In selecting toys and playthings for young children, it is important to think about what the children are capable of doing and how they can explore the objects safely and learn from their play.

- Be open to providing the beautiful junk and common objects that will intrigue and delight a young child.

Talking With Children as They Play

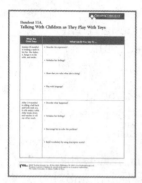

☐ "Child Planning Form"

☐ Handout 11A

☐ *The Creative Curriculum*, pp. 302–304

Preparation

Review pages 302–306 in *The Creative Curriculum*.

Prepare handout 11A.

Introduction

Make the following points:

- Your responsiveness and engagement will fascinate a very young child more than almost any toy.

- When you show a real interest in what children are doing, you convey that their actions have value.

- Talking with and supporting children's efforts can really enhance their play experiences.

Activity

Have participants review pages 302–304, which describe what teachers might say as children of different ages play with toys.

Refer participants to handout 11A, "Talking With Children as They Play With Toys." Instruct participants to work with the people at their tables to give examples for each type of comment. Encourage them to write what they would say to each of the four children.

Invite each group to share the comments they wrote for one of the children. After the group has shared its comments, invite the other groups to add ideas they developed for that child.

Refer participants to the "Child Planning Form." Ask them to discuss and record something they learned about each child and how they would use what they learned to plan.

Summary

Make the following points:

- Playing with toys becomes a richer, more meaningful experience when adults talk with children about what they are doing.

- Your interactions with children provide an opportunity to find out what interests each child and to use what you learn to plan your program.

Imitating and Pretending

Workshops

⚙ WORKSHOP	🔑 KEY POINTS	🗒 MATERIALS	⏱ TIME (minutes)
Props Across the Ages (p. 228)	A few well-chosen props and objects can inspire children to imitate actions they have seen and, as they get older, to replay experiences and events.	☐ A variety of simple props ☐ *The Creative Curriculum,* pp. 311–313	30–45
Encouraging Imitation and Pretend Play (p. 230)	Adults can teach children how to imitate and pretend by being playful, repeating the gestures and sounds children make, singing and acting out songs and fingerplays, pretending along with them, and asking questions.	☐ Handout 12A. Responding to Each Child ☐ *The Creative Curriculum,* pp. 47–57 and 319, and Appendix, p. 424, "Goals and Objectives at a Glance"	45

Props Across the Ages

☐ Variety of simple props

☐ *The Creative Curriculum,* pp. 311–313

Preparation

Review pages 311–313 in *The Creative Curriculum*.

Ask participants to bring in one prop or object that encourages young children to imitate and pretend.

Collect a variety of props and objects to supplement what participants bring, and place some on each group's table. Examples of these props or objects include rattles, stuffed animals, dolls, hats, boots, cars, small purses and tote bags, play telephones, plastic tools, plastic or rubber animals, and cooking utensils.

Introduction

Make the following points:

- Infants, toddlers, and twos begin imitating and pretending at a very early age.

- A few well-chosen props and objects can inspire children to imitate actions they have seen and, as they get older, to replay experiences and events.

Activity

Give the following instructions:

- Look over the props and objects on your table and talk about how children of different ages might use them.

- Sort them into age categories: What would appeal to young infants, mobile infants, toddlers, and 2-year-olds?

- Are any of the props and objects appropriate for more than one age group?

- Review pages 311–313 in *The Creative Curriculum* and discuss what other props might be appropriate for each age-group.

Discuss ideas for displaying props and objects that encourage imitation and pretend play.

Summary

- Very young children imitate actions they see and sounds they hear if encouraged to do so. The very best props are your interest and enthusiasm.

- A few simple props, especially ones that relate to family life and other common experiences of infants, toddlers, and twos, will inspire children to imitate and pretend.

- Display props attractively and conveniently so children can find and use them.

Encouraging Imitation and Pretend Play

☐ Handout 12A

☐ *The Creative Curriculum*, , pp. 47–57 and 319, and Appendix, p. 424

Preparation

Review pages 47–57 and 314–319, and the appendix, page 424, "Goals and Objectives at a Glance," of *The Creative Curriculum*.

Introduction

Make the following points:

- Adults can teach children how to imitate and pretend by being playful, repeating the gestures and sounds children make, singing and acting out songs and fingerplays, pretending along with them, and asking questions.

- The *Developmental Continuum* will help you determine each child's level and how you can respond in ways that support and extend learning.

Activity

Refer participants to page 319 in *The Creative Curriculum* and have them review the sample of four teachers' observations, what each teacher thought about, and how each teacher responded.

Refer participants to handout 12A, "Responding to Each Child," and give the following instructions:

- Work with a partner and discuss each of the sample observation notes on the handout.

- Referring to the goals and objectives on page 424 in *The Creative Curriculum*, record—in the middle column of handout 12A—any objectives you think are related.

- Talk about what you might do and say to respond to each child in ways that encourage imitation and pretend play.

When participants have finished, ask them to turn to pages 47–57 in *The Creative Curriculum*, find two objectives they identified, and talk about what step they think the child might be on. Ask:

- How would the *Developmental Continuum* help you to respond to the child appropriately?

- How would it help you plan your program?

Summary

Make the following points:

- Your observations of children enable you to determine what interests a child. Then you can respond in ways that extend and deepen the child's experience.

- One observation is never sufficient to determine what step a child is on for each objective. Several observations, over time, are needed.

- Your encouragement and your active involvement with children as they imitate and pretend help them develop these very important play skills.

Enjoying Stories and Books

Workshops

⚙ WORKSHOP	🔑 KEY POINTS	📄 MATERIALS	⏱ TIME (minutes)
Best Sellers for Babies (p. 234)	Reading aloud and sharing your pleasure in language and stories are some of the most important experiences you can offer young children.	☐ Children's books for each table ☐ Chart paper ☐ Markers ☐ *The Creative Curriculum,* pp. 326–328 and 331–332	45
Making Books for Children (p. 236)	You can make many kinds of books to add to your book collection.	☐ Zipper-lock plastic bags ☐ Construction paper or card stock ☐ Hole punch ☐ Scissors ☐ Ribbon or yarn ☐ Magazines and/or catalogs ☐ Glue sticks or transparent tape ☐ Handout 13A. Making Books for Children	45–60
Sharing Thoughts About Enjoying Stories and Books (p. 238)	Developing a bookbag lending library is a wonderful way to build a strong connection between families and your program and to encourage families to read to their children every day.	☐ Children's books ☐ Handout 13B. Enjoying Stories and Books With Your Child ☐ Handout 13C. Enjoying Stories and Books With Your Child: Sample ☐ *The Creative Curriculum,* pp. 331–335 and 341	60

Best Sellers for Babies

- [ ] Children's books
- [ ] Chart Paper
- [ ] Markers
- [ ] *The Creative Curriculum*, pp. 326–328 and 331–332

Preparation

Review pages 325–332 in *The Creative Curriculum*.

Gather a variety of books for infants, toddlers, and twos. If possible, ask participants to bring one of their children's favorite books to the training.

Introduction

Make the following points:

- Reading with infants, toddlers, and twos can be the most treasured time of your day.

- Keep the following in mind when selecting books for infants, toddlers, and twos:

  - Select high-quality books that you will enjoy sharing.

  - Keep the children's developmental levels in mind.

  - Look for books that respect diversity and support inclusion.

  - Include homemade books, personalized for a child or the children in your group.

Activity

Ask participants what books the children like best and why they think these books are so popular.

Tell participants that they are going to be a book club for very young children. Like all book clubs, their first job is to select a good book for everyone to read.

Put picture books on each table and invite participants to share the books they brought. Give the following instructions:

- Refer to the criteria for selecting books on pages 326–328 in *The Creative Curriculum*.

- Look at the collection on your table and, together with the others at your table, select one book to recommend as the book club selection.

- Be prepared to present and defend your group's selection to the other book club members. In doing so, you should say whether the book is appropriate for young infants, mobile infants, toddlers, or twos, and why you think it is the best choice.

After all the groups have chosen a book, invite each group to present its selection to the entire group.

Explain that the next thing that book clubs do is read and discuss the book. Refer participants to the general tips for reading stories to children on pages 331–332. Ask them how they could make reading the book they selected an interactive experience and how they could use the book to extend children's learning.

Summary

Make the following points:

- Reading aloud and sharing your pleasure in language and stories are some of the most important experiences you can offer infants, toddlers, and twos.

- Make sure that you read to every child, every day, either individually or in a small group.

- Your interactions as you snuggle together with a book, your enthusiasm, the way you bring a story to life through dramatic reading, and your interesting questions make story reading special for young children.

- Children develop a foundation for literacy when they regularly hear books read aloud and have opportunities to explore them firsthand.

Making Books for Children

- ☐ Zipper-lock plastic bags
- ☐ Construction paper or card stock
- ☐ Hole punch
- ☐ Scissors
- ☐ Ribbon or yarn
- ☐ Magazines and/or catalogs
- ☐ Glue sticks or transparent tape
- ☐ Handout 13A

Preparation

Review pages 325–335 in *The Creative Curriculum*.

If possible, ask each participant to bring in a picture of something of interest to infants and toddlers.

Cut construction paper or card stock to fit as pages inside zipper-lock bags. (Rolling the paper slightly helps to place it in the bags.)

Display or distribute the other bookmaking materials.

Prepare handout 13A, "Making Books for Children."

Practice following the steps in handout 13A so that you can demonstrate them easily.

Introduction

Make the following points:

- Your book collection should include some homemade books.

- Young children, especially toddlers and 2-year-olds, love to see pictures and hear stories about themselves and their families.

- You can make many kinds of homemade books: books about children and their families; books about a shared experience; books about simple objects and concepts; and books filled with things to touch or smell.

Activity

Invite participants to make homemade books. Set out materials and demonstrate the steps for making zipper-lock bag books (see handout 13A, "Making Books for Children"). Allow time for participants to assemble their books. When all of the groups have finished, have participants share their books with others in the group.

Ask participants to share other ways to make safe books for infants and toddlers. Distribute and review handout 13A, "Making Books for Children," for additional instructions and ideas.

Summary

- Homemade books can include pictures of children and their families, or children's favorite things.

- You can give homemade books as gifts to families to share with their children.

Trainer's Note: You can have additional workshops to make other books that are explained on the handout. Making homemade books is also an excellent activity to do with families.

Sharing Thoughts About Enjoying Stories and Books

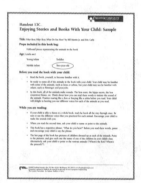

☐ Children's books

☐ Handout 13B

☐ Handout 13C
(optional)

Preparation

Review pages 331–335 and 341 in *The Creative Curriculum*.

Copy handout 13B, "Enjoying Stories and Books With Your Child," on card stock.

Copy handout 13C, "Enjoying Stories and Books With Your Child: Sample."

Introduction

Make the following points:

- Encourage families to read and tell stories to their child every day.

- Although the words and pictures in books are important, it is the special time that families spend with their children as they read aloud that lets children know how much families value these activities.

Activity

Ask participants to imagine that their program's staff is about to embark on an exciting project. At the last staff meeting, all of the teachers agreed to make family literacy a focus for the year. The plan is to create a lending library of bookbags that can be sent home with the infants, toddlers, and twos in your program. Each bookbag will contain a high-quality children's book for families to read to their child. An activity card will accompany the book and will feature suggestions for reading the book aloud, asking questions, and pursuing follow-up activities.

Give the following instructions:

- Working in groups of three, select one of the books on your table. Decide what age-group to think about.

- Read the book and think about ideas you would give families for reading the book with their child.

- Complete handout 13B, "Enjoying Stories and Books With Your Child," by writing tips for families.

Trainer's Note: You may want to distribute and review handout 13C, "Enjoying Stories and Books With Your Child: Sample."

- Think about what kinds of props to include in the bookbag (see the example on handout 13C).

Allow time for each group to complete the handout. Invite participants to share their ideas for the bookbags and their thoughts on how to implement this project at their program.

Summary

- Many families enjoy reading books with their children. They may already have favorite books and times, such as bedtime, when they routinely read to their children.

- One way to build a strong connection between families and your program, and to encourage families to read to their children every day, is to develop a bookbag lending library.

Trainer's Note: You now have the materials to start a bookbag lending library for your program. Collect the bookbags from this workshop, with their books and activity pages. Put them in your family resource area and develop a system that enables families to borrow the bookbags.

Connecting With Music and Movement

Workshops

 WORKSHOP	 KEY POINTS	 MATERIALS	TIME (minutes)
Music Our Way (p. 242)	Music affects our emotions and inspires movement. You can encourage families to share their musical preferences, special songs, and the music of their cultures.	☐ *The Creative Curriculum*, p. 355	50
Music for the Ages (p. 244)	Understanding how children develop and learn can help you provide appropriate music and movement experiences for infants, toddlers, and twos.	☐ Chart paper ☐ Markers ☐ Handout 14A. Music and Movement: Strategy Cards ☐ *The Creative Curriculum*, pp. 348–351	60
Music and Movement: Responding to and Planning for Each Child (p. 246)	As you observe children during music and movement experiences, consider what each child is learning and how you would respond. Based on this information, complete the "Child Planning Form."	☐ Handout 14B. Using Your Observations to Plan Music and Movement Experiences ☐ *The Creative Curriculum*, pp. 352–353	45

Music Our Way

☐ *The Creative Curriculum*, p. 355

Preparation

Review pages 344–346 and 355 in *The Creative Curriculum*.

Introduction

Make the following points:

- Most people enjoy listening to, creating, and moving to music.

- Music affects our emotions and inspires movement. Music can be relaxing and invigorating, calming and exciting. Choosing musical selections thoughtfully helps to ensure that they suit children's changing moods and interests.

- You don't have to be able to carry a tune, play an instrument, or dance like a professional to incorporate music and movement into your room.

- What's important is to share your enjoyment of music and movement with the children in your group.

- You can encourage families to share their musical preferences, special songs, and the music of their cultures.

Activity

Give the following instructions:

- Imagine that you are stuck in an elevator with music playing in the background. Take a moment to think about how the music is making your feel.

- In this elevator, you are in control. You can have any music that you want. Imagine that a recording of your favorite kind of music, your favorite song, or your favorite musician is playing. Listen for a few moments. How do you feel now?

Discuss each of the following questions briefly:

- What role does music play in the environment?

- How does music affect our moods?

- How do you set up your environment for music and movement?

- When and how do you use music in your room?

- How do you use music to connect children's homes, families, cultures, and languages to the program?

Remind participants that each experience chapter in *The Creative Curriculum* ends with a letter that shares information with families about why the experience is important.

Give the following instructions:

> Work with your group to think of a way to share with families why music and movement are important. Think about the key points you want to make. Rather than write a letter for families, come up with a way of using music and movement to share the information.

Tell participants that they will have about 15 minutes to create their music and movement presentation for families, and that each group will have 5 minutes to present it to the whole group.

After all groups have presented, refer participants to "Sharing Thoughts About Music and Movement" on page 355 in *The Creative Curriculum*. Then summarize the important points of the presentations.

Summary

- Music affects our emotions and inspires movement.

- Music can be relaxing and invigorating, calming and exciting.

- Choosing musical selections thoughtfully helps ensure that they suit children's changing moods and interests.

- You can use music to connect children's homes, families, cultures, and languages to the program.

WORKSHOP

Music for the Ages

☐ Chart paper
☐ Markers
☐ Handout 14A
☐ *The Creative Curriculum*, pp. 348–351

Preparation

Review pages 343–351 in *The Creative Curriculum*.

Copy handout 14A, "Music and Movement: Strategy Cards," on card stock so that you have a set for each group. Cut the cards and mix them up.

Introduction

Make the following points:

- Music and movement are natural parts of children's lives.

- Understanding how children develop and learn can help you provide appropriate music and movement experiences for infants, toddlers, and twos.

Activity

Ask participants to stand, sing, and move with you as you lead them in three songs.

- Sing "Rock-a-Bye, Baby," or another lullaby, and ask participants to sing and sway with you.

- Next, invite participants to join in as you sing a nursery rhyme appropriate for mobile infants and toddlers, such as "Pat-a-Cake," or a musical fingerplay, such as "The Itsy-Bitsy Spider."

- Finally, sing an activity song, such as "If You're Happy and You Know It," that you might use with toddlers and twos.

Ask participants about the differences in tempo and when they might use each type of song. Point out that the tempo of a lullaby is similar to an adult heartbeat, which is why a lullaby is so soothing. Note that the tempos of nursery rhymes and fingerplays are different from that of a lullaby, and that activity songs for toddlers and twos have an even more upbeat tempo.

Put a set of "Music and Movement Strategy Cards" on each table. Tell participants to read each of the cards, discuss the strategies, and decide whether they are appropriate for young infants, mobile infants, toddlers, or twos. When they have finished, have them look at pages 348–351 in *The Creative Curriculum*.

Divide participants into groups according to the age of the children with whom they work (i.e., young infants, mobile infants, toddlers, or twos). Instruct them to keep the strategies in mind as they think of an example of one of the following music and movement experiences for their age-group:

- Sounds or instruments

- Song

- Gross motor activity

- Fine motor activity

Allow groups to work for about 15 minutes. While they are working, distribute a piece of chart paper and several markers to each group and ask participants to write their ideas on the chart paper. Invite each group to teach its activity to the entire group. After each group's presentation, lead a discussion about how the activity could be modified for children of a different age.

Summary

- Children of all ages connect with music and movement.

- Include music and movement experiences every day.

Music and Movement:
Responding to and Planning for Each Child

☐ Handout 14B

☐ *The Creative Curriculum,* pp. 352–353

Preparation

Review pages 95–97 and 352–354 in *The Creative Curriculum.*

Copy handout 14B, "Using Your Observations to Plan Music and Movement Experiences."

Introduction

Make the following points:

- As you observe children during music and movement experiences, think about the goals, objectives, and steps of the *Developmental Continuum.*

- Consider what each child is learning and how you might respond.

- Use your observation notes to help you complete the "Child Planning Form."

Activity

Tell participants that in this activity they will use what they have learned during a music and movement experience about a young infant, a mobile infant, a toddler, and a 2-year-old to complete a "Child Planning Form."

Remind participants that the "Child Planning Form" is used every week to record what they know about a child's changing interests and abilities, so that they can use the information to plan appropriate experiences for that child.

Distribute handout 14B, "Using Your Observations to Plan Music and Movement Experiences." Review the first row, which includes an observation note made during a musical experience for 4-month-old Julio. It also reports his teacher Linda's reflection and response.

Instruct participants to complete the "Child Planning Form" box for Julio on handout 14B. Answers should be based on Linda's observation, reflection, and response.

Invite a few participants to share their answers. Then instruct them to read the three other scenarios and complete the "Child Planning Form" boxes for the three other children.

When participants have finished, refer them to the completed chart on pages 352–353 in *The Creative Curriculum*, including the examples of using the "Child Planning Form."

Summary

Make the following points:

- Your observations during children's experiences, including music and movement, can help you plan appropriate experiences for each child in your group.

- You use the "Child Planning Form" to record this information and your individualized plans for a child.

Creating With Art

Workshops

⚙ WORKSHOP	🔑 KEY POINTS	📄 MATERIALS	⏱ TIME (minutes)
Art Studio (p. 250)	Art for infants, toddlers, and twos is largely a sensory experience. Young children are interested in what different materials are like and what they can do with them. Different age-groups use the same art materials in different ways.	☐ Variety of art materials ☐ *The Creative Curriculum*, p. 358	45
"You're Using Your Fingers to Spread the Paint!" (p. 254)	Talking with children about the process as they create art validates their work, encourages their involvement, supports their thinking, and helps them learn vocabulary that relates to what they are doing and feeling.	☐ Large photograph of a flower ☐ Samples of children's artwork ☐ Chart paper ☐ Markers ☐ White paper, 8½" x 11" ☐ Crayons ☐ Handout 15A. Sample Artwork ☐ *The Creative Curriculum,* pp. 366–369	60
Inappropriate Art Activities (p. 258)	Any art activity that focuses on a finished product rather than on the creative process is inappropriate for infants, toddlers, and twos.	☐ Chart paper ☐ Markers	50

Art Studio

- ☐ Variety of art materials
- ☐ *The Creative Curriculum*, p. 358

Preparation

Review pages 357–365 in *The Creative Curriculum*.

Collect a variety of art materials and set them up in stations around the room.

Here are some suggestions for art stations and related materials:

- Painting with water: water, paint brushes, and large sheets of construction paper

- Fabric bin: swatches of fabrics with different textures, colors, and patterns in a plastic tub or basket

- Paper pile: a variety of different kinds of paper, such as construction, tissue, and watercolor paper and card stock.

- Drawing: paper and fat crayons

- Bubble art: a few containers of bubbles with wands and sheets of construction paper (blow bubbles toward the paper; when they pop, the bubbles make interesting marks on the paper)

- Sticky collage: a large sheet of contact paper (taped on the table with the sticky side up) and a selection of collage materials

- Molding: playdough in a variety of colors, cloud dough, or baker's clay

- Finger painting: cafeteria trays, finger paints, and paper

- Golf-ball painting—a few golf balls, shallow dishes of paint, a few 9" x 13" metal baking pans, and paper sized to fit in the baking pans

Introduction

Make the following points:

- Art for infants, toddlers, and twos is largely a sensory experience.

- Young children are interested in investigating different materials and discovering what they can do with them. They are not intent on making a product.

- In this workshop, you will explore a variety of art materials and consider how children of different ages use them.

Activity

Give the following instructions:

- Several art stations are set up around the room. On your own, circulate around the room and explore the various art experiences. Try each experience.

- Choose an age-group (young infants, mobile infants, toddlers, or twos) to keep in mind while you work and play. As you use the materials, think about how a child in your age-group might use them.

Allow enough time for each participant to experience all of the art stations. Then give these instructions:

- Find a partner who works with children of the same age as the children you teach.

Trainer's Note: If you have a large group, you may want participants to work in small groups instead of partnerships.

- With your partner, select an art station that is appropriate for your age-group.

- At the station, briefly explore the materials and discuss how a child in your age-group might use them.

- Next, discuss how the art experience promotes development and learning. While you work, use page 358 in *The Creative Curriculum* as a reference.

- You will have 15 minutes to explore and discuss.

After the participants are finished with their discussions, ask each partnership to share their ideas with the large group.

Summary

Make the following points:

- The everyday art experiences you offer infants, toddlers, and twos build a foundation for both appreciating and creating art.

- Art for infants, toddlers, and twos is largely a sensory experience. By providing a variety of art experiences for young children, you help children discover that certain materials feel interesting and are fun to use.

- Through art experiences, children also learn that they can control and make marks with a variety of tools and materials. This builds a foundation for learning to write.

- Older twos begin to understand that the pictures, models, and constructions they make can represent people and things.

Notes:

"You're Using Your Fingers to Spread the Paint!"

- ☐ Large photograph of a flower
- ☐ Samples of children's artwork
- ☐ Chart paper
- ☐ Markers
- ☐ White paper, 8½" x 11"
- ☐ Crayons
- ☐ Handout 15A
- ☐ *The Creative Curriculum,* pp. 366–369

Preparation

Review pages 366–369 in *The Creative Curriculum*.

Collect a variety of samples of children's artwork. Before the workshop, you may want to ask participants to bring a few samples with them.

Display the artwork around the room. Hang a sheet of chart paper by each piece.

Introduction

- Art experiences are a wonderful way for infants, toddlers, and twos to develop their social/emotional, physical, cognitive, and language skills.

- When you provide a variety of art experiences for young children, they discover that materials feel interesting and are fun to use.

- The everyday art experiences you offer infants, toddlers, and twos build a foundation for both appreciating and creating through art.

Activity 1

Guide participants through the following example of how *not* to respond to children's art:

- Tell the participants that they are going to participate in a fun art activity.

- Give each participant a piece of paper and each table a set of crayons.

- Show the participants the photo of a flower. Instruct them to draw a flower that looks like the one in the photograph.

Circulate around the room, looking at and commenting on participants' artwork as follows:

- If the participants say it is too hard, tell them that they need to stop complaining because art time is fun.

- If they talk to each other, tell them that there is no talking during art time and that they should be concentrating on their drawing.

- If someone at a table takes two or more crayons, tell them that they may only use one crayon at a time and that they must share the materials with the other people at the table.

- Arbitrarily pick a few people and tell them that their pictures are beautiful. Hold the "beautiful" pictures up and tell the rest of the group how perfect those pictures are.

- Pick a couple of people and tell them that their pictures do not look like the one in the photo and that they need to try harder. (You may want to ask these participants ahead of time if they would feel comfortable participating in this way.)

- Pick a few people to tell them that their picture is fine, nice, or okay. Give this feedback in a nonchalant tone of voice.

After a few minutes of drawing, tell everyone that it is cleanup time. Collect the pictures. In the front of the room, hang the pictures you called "beautiful." Leave the rest in a pile on a table.

Debrief the activity by asking participants the following questions:

- How did you feel about yourself during the art experience?

- How did you feel about me?

- How did you feel about your ability to create art?

- How did those of you who were told they drew a beautiful picture feel while you were being complimented?

- How did those of you who did not receive praise feel about your work while I was complimenting the other participants? How did you feel about the participants who made the beautiful art?

Make the following points:

- There are some differences between the kinds of art experiences you offer infants and those you plan for toddlers and twos, and the process of using art materials is more important than the product that children create.

- Praising children's art or making judgments about their work can make children feel uncomfortable about their art. It can also create competition and may encourage children to create art to please you rather than to enjoy the process, themselves.

- Talking to children about what they are doing as they create art validates their work, encourages their involvement, supports their critical thinking, and helps them learn vocabulary that relates to what they are doing and feeling.

Activity 2

Instruct participants to review the bullet points on pages 366–369 in *The Creative Curriculum*.

Show handout 15A, "Sample Artwork." Explain to participants that, rather than telling the child who created this art that her picture is beautiful, you would say, "I see you made big, round lines."

Ask volunteers to contribute something else that they might say to the child about her art.

Point out the children's artwork displayed throughout the room.

Distribute a set of markers to each table. Give the following instructions:

- Choose a marker.

- Walk around the room and look at each piece of art.

- Think of something that you could say to the children about their art that validates their work, encourages involvement, supports critical thinking, and helps them learn the words that relate to what they are doing and feeling.

- Record your ideas on the chart paper next to each work of art.

After all of the participants have had a chance to record what they could say about each work of art, have them come back together as a large group.

Pick a few of the charts and review the participants' responses with the group. If any responses are inappropriate (e.g., "I really like your picture."), ask how the comment could be made more appropriate.

Summary

Make the following points:

- For young children, the process of creating with art is important, not the finished product.

- Share in each child's enjoyment of the process and focus on responding to what each child is doing.

- Commenting on what the child is experiencing and doing validates his work, encourages his involvement, supports his critical thinking, and helps him learn the words that relate to what he is doing and feeling.

- Your genuine interest in what a child is doing makes any experience, including art, both more enjoyable and an opportunity for the child to learn.

Inappropriate Art Activities

☐ Chart paper
☐ Markers

Preparation:

Review page 370 in *The Creative Curriculum*.

On each of six sheets of chart paper, write one of the art activities for children under age 3 that are listed on page 370 in *The Creative Curriculum*.

Introduction

Make the following points:

- Any art activity that focuses on a finished product rather than on the creative process is inappropriate for infants, toddlers, and twos.

- Very young children are not yet developmentally able to create representative art.

Activity

Have participants form six groups. Give each group a piece of chart paper with one of the art activities written at the top.

Give the following instructions:

- With the people in your group, discuss why the activity written on your chart paper is inappropriate for infants, toddlers, and twos.

- Record your ideas on the paper.

After 5–10 minutes, give the following instructions:

- Plan a response that your group would give to a family member who asked you why you do not offer that particular activity to the children.

- In your response, include the reason why the activity is inappropriate, an example of an activity that you would do as an alternative, why the alternative activity is appropriate, and how the alternative activity supports children's development and learning.

Allow enough time for the groups to generate a response. Have each small group share their chart and their response with the large group, and invite additional discussion.

Summary

Make the following points:

- For very young children, art is a sensorimotor experience that builds a foundation for creativity and art appreciation.

- The process of creating art is more important than what the child produces.

Tasting and Preparing Food

Workshops

⚙ WORKSHOP	🔑 KEY POINTS	📄 MATERIALS	🕐 TIME (minutes)
Tasting and Preparing Food: What Children Are Learning (p. 262)	Knowing about child development will help you plan appropriate food experiences that help the children in your group develop social/emotional, physical, cognitive, and language skills.	☐ Bowls, plastic spoons, different kinds of baby food, spices, sour cream, yogurt or cottage cheese, grated cheese ☐ Handout 16A. Tasting and Preparing Food: What Children Are Learning ☐ *The Creative Curriculum*, pp. 163 and 380–382	60
Planning Tasting and Food Preparation Experiences for Each Child and for the Group (p. 266)	Use the "Child Planning Form" and the "Group Planning Form" to plan food experiences based on your observations of children's interests and abilities.	☐ Handout 16B. Planning for Each Child and for the Group	45

Tasting and Preparing Food: What Children Are Learning

☐ Utensils and food

☐ Handout 16A

☐ *The Creative Curriculum*, pp. 163 and 380–382

Preparation

Review pages 163 and 376–383 in *The Creative Curriculum*.

Set out utensils and food on each table as follows:

For each pair:

- A small bowl
- Plastic spoons

For each table:

- A small container of sour cream, yogurt, or cottage cheese
- Grated cheese
- Spices such as cinnamon, nutmeg, thyme, or oregano
- A variety of jars of baby food with the labels removed

Introduction

Make the following points:

- Tasting and preparing food are part of everyday experiences with infants, toddlers, and twos.

- During this experience, children have opportunities to strengthen their social/emotional, physical, cognitive, and language skills.

- Knowing about child development will help you select appropriate materials and plan appropriate food experiences for the children in your group.

Activity

Tell participants that, in this activity, they will have two experiences with tasting and preparing food. The first is similar to the exciting experience a young infant has each time a new food is introduced. The second is a food preparation activity appropriate for mobile infants, toddlers, or twos.

Ask participants to open the baby food jars that are on their tables. Invite them to pass the jars around the table, allowing each person to look at the colors and smell the food. See if participants can guess what each food is. Invite them to taste the different foods (no double dipping, please).

Refer participants to page 163 in *The Creative Curriculum* and ask them to read the section "Talking With Infants, Toddlers, and Twos."

Ask:

- If you were feeding one of these foods to a young infant, how would you describe the experience to the child?

- How might you introduce the names of the foods; the adjectives that describe the smells, tastes, and textures; and the verbs that tell what the child is doing?

Conduct a brief discussion.

Tell participants that now they will have a food experience that is appropriate for mobile infants, toddlers, and twos. Children of these ages may enjoy making dips for snacks by mixing grated cheese or spices with sour cream, yogurt, or cottage cheese. Give the following instructions:

- Make a dip with your partner, using the materials on your table.

- As you are making the dip, think about what children might be learning while making the dip and what you would say to children to stretch their thinking and extend their learning.

Conduct a discussion of the experience with the group.

Distribute handout 16A, "Tasting and Preparing Food: What Children Are Learning" and give the following instructions:

- Find a partner who works with children who are the same age as those in your group.

- Read one of the following pages of *The Creative Curriculum:*

  - If you work with young infants, read page 380.

  - If you work with mobile infants, read page 381.

  - If you work with toddlers or twos, read page 382.

- Working with your partner, select one of the tasting and preparing experiences listed for your children's age-group. (Don't select making a dip!) Then complete the handout with your partner.

Invite one or two pairs from each age-group to talk about the tasting and preparing experience they selected and their responses to the questions in the handout.

Summary

- While they are tasting and preparing food, children are learning about themselves and others, about moving, about the world, and about communicating.

- Food experiences for young infants involve both tasting foods and building relationships with those who feed them.

- Food experiences for mobile infants include shaking, dipping, stirring, and mashing. Mobile infants enjoy being involved in preparing their snacks.

- Toddlers and twos can have food experiences that involve spreading, pouring, slicing, whisking, squeezing, and garnishing. Children this age can take a more active role in preparing foods.

- When you observe children and see what skills they are using and developing, you can respond in ways that stretch children's thinking and extend their learning.

Notes:

WORKSHOP

Planning Tasting and Food Preparation Experiences for Each Child and for the Group

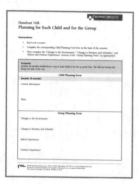

☐ Handout 16B

Preparation

Review pages 385–386 in *The Creative Curriculum.*

Copy handout 16B, "Planning for Each Child and for the Group."

Introduction

Make the following points:

- As you observe children during tasting and food preparation experiences, think about what you are learning about each child's interests and abilities.

- Use the "Child Planning Form" area on the handout to summarize up-to-date information about each child and to plan for each child as an individual.

- Use the "Group Planning Form" area to use what you know about individual children to plan for your group.

Activity

Distribute handout 16B, "Planning for Each Child and for the Group," and give the following instructions:

- Read each scenario on the handout.

- On the basis of the scenario, complete the corresponding "Child Planning Form" area on the handout.

- Then complete the "Changes to the Environment," "Changes to Routines and Schedules," and "Indoor and Outdoor Experiences" sections of the "Group Planning Form" area on the handout (as appropriate).

Allow about 15 minutes for participants to complete the activity.

Ask the following questions:

- What current information did you have for each child?

- What did you plan for the child on the basis of that information?

- How did you complete the "Group Planning Form"?

Summary

- The "Child Planning Form" and the "Group Planning Form" help you plan for each child and for the group on the basis of your observations and current information about each child.

Exploring Sand and Water

Workshops

⬡ WORKSHOP	🔑 KEY POINTS	🗒 MATERIALS	🕑 TIME (minutes)
Setting Up Sand and Water Play (p. 270)	Sand and water are soothing materials for infants, toddlers, and twos. A small amount of sand or water and a few simple props are all children need to have an enjoyable experience.	☐ Chart paper ☐ Markers of five different colors ☐ Tape ☐ Materials for sand and water play ☐ *The Creative Curriculum*, Appendix, p. 424, "Goals and Objectives at a Glance"	45
Obstacles and Solutions: Successful Sand and Water Play (p. 274)	Although sand and water experiences can be messy, teachers can minimize problems by planning ahead and participating in children's play.	☐ Chart paper ☐ Markers ☐ Handout 17A. Obstacles and Solutions ☐ *The Creative Curriculum*, pp. 389–401	45

Setting Up Sand and Water Play

- ☐ Chart paper
- ☐ Markers of five different colors
- ☐ Tape
- ☐ Materials for sand and water play
- ☐ *The Creative Curriculum*, Appendix, p. 424

Preparation

Review pages 391–393 in *The Creative Curriculum*.

Prepare a sheet of chart paper for each group. For each sheet, use a marker to divide the sheet into four sections and label each section with one of the following headings:

1. What Age-Group and Why

2. Health and Safety Considerations

3. What You Might Say and Do

4. Related Goals and Objectives

At tables on which participants can explore sand and water, set up stations with materials to provide the following types of experiences:

- A basin with a few inches of sand and a collection of small objects such as coffee scoops, small rakes and hoes, small plastic animal and people figures, straws, funnels, and shells.

- A basin with a few inches of water and small objects such as coffee scoops, funnels, plastic boats and fish, ladles, scoops, and rubber ducks.

- A cafeteria tray with a small amount of sand and a small rake and hoe.

- A cafeteria tray with a small amount of water.

- Bubble-blowing solution on a plate with straws, plastic berry containers, and shapes made from wire to produce different kinds of bubbles.

Near each station, post one sheet of the prepared chart paper.

Introduction

Ask participants to think back to when they were very young children.

- What memories do you have of playing with sand and water?

- Visualize yourself there. What words come to mind to describe your experiences?

- Do you still enjoy sand and water experiences as an adult?

Make the following points:

- Sand and water are soothing materials for children and for adults.

- Experiences with sand and water should be readily available to children.

- Sand and water play support children's development and learning.

Activity

Have participants count off by fives to form five groups.

Provide each group with a different colored marker and give the following instructions:

- Spend 5 minutes at each of the stations, playing with the materials.

- Talk about which age-group you would offer these materials to, any safety or health considerations you would need to address, what you might say and do to make it a meaningful experience for children, and what goals and objectives could be addressed.

- Have one person record your ideas on the chart paper.

- I will give you a 1-minute warning before it's time to move to the next station.

When all five groups have been to each station and recorded their ideas, allow time for them to read the chart papers to see what other groups recorded. Write down any interesting ideas you want to highlight in summarizing the experience.

Gather all of the participants and ask:

- What were these experiences like for you?

- Is there anything you would like to try with your children that you hadn't thought of before?

- Turn to the appendix, p. 424, "Goals and Objectives at a Glance," in *The Creative Curriculum*. Look over the goals and objectives. How many different objectives might you address through these kinds of experiences?

Summary

Make the following points:

- You don't need a lot of materials to provide sand and water experiences for very young children.

- Your involvement with children expands and enriches the experience for them as they play with sand and water.

- To support their development and learning, encourage children to explore with sand and water indoors as well as outdoors.

Notes:

WORKSHOP

Obstacles and Solutions: Successful Sand and Water Play

☐ Chart paper
☐ Markers
☐ Handout 17A
☐ *The Creative Curriculum*, pp. 389–401

Preparation

Review pages 389–401 in *The Creative Curriculum*.

Make one copy of handout 17A, "Obstacles and Solutions," for each participant.

Introduction

Make the following points:

- When infant, toddlers, and twos explore sand and water, it can be a bit messy. For this reason, some teachers do not offer children these experiences on a regular basis.

- In this workshop, we will consider some of the obstacles to successful sand and water play and how they can be addressed.

Activity

Ask participants to describe challenges or obstacles that teachers face in providing successful sand and water play. Record their responses on chart paper, adding any of the following obstacles that are not mentioned.

- Children's clothes get wet.

- Parents complain if their children come home with sand in their hair.

- Water breeds germs, so the children might get sick.

- The children make a mess, and we don't have time to clean it up.

- Children or adults can slip and fall on a wet or sandy floor.

- The custodian complains that sand ruins the floor.

- My co-teacher doesn't understand the value of sand and water play for this age-group.

- It's fun for children, but they aren't really learning anything.

- The children get bored pretty quickly.

Refer participants to handout 17A, "Obstacles and Solutions," and give the following instructions:

- In the left-hand column, write those obstacles from our list that you must overcome to provide successful sand and water experiences for your children.

- Think of some possible solutions for each one. Refer to pages 389–401 in *The Creative Curriculum* for more ideas.

- Take turns sharing your ideas with the people at your table.

Summary

Make the following points:

- Taking a few precautions can eliminate most problems associated with sand and water experiences for young children.

- Children should always be supervised when playing with sand and water.

- By participating in the play, you can extend children's learning.

Going Outdoors

Workshops

⬡ WORKSHOP	⚷ KEY POINTS	▤ MATERIALS	⏱ TIME (minutes)
The Joy of Outdoor Experiences (p. 278)	Making discoveries outdoors is exciting and invigorating for young children, who can learn a lot from firsthand experiences with nature.	☐ Chart paper ☐ Markers ☐ Real and artificial leaves, construction paper cutouts of leaves, and coloring book pictures of leaves ☐ Crayons ☐ *The Creative Curriculum,* Appendix, p. 424, "Goals and Objectives at a Glance"	60
Keeping Children Safe and Healthy Outdoors (p. 280)	Constant supervision and daily monitoring of the outdoor area is essential to ensuring children's safety and health.	☐ Chart paper ☐ Markers ☐ Masking tape ☐ *The Creative Curriculum,* pp. 406–408	30
Designing Your Ideal Outdoor Area (p. 282)	The more appropriate and appealing the outdoor area is for children, and the more you are involved with them, the richer their outdoor experiences will be.	☐ Chart paper ☐ Markers: A set for each table ☐ Masking tape ☐ *The Creative Curriculum,* pp. 409–420	60

WORKSHOP

The Joy of Outdoor Experiences

- ☐ Chart paper
- ☐ Markers
- ☐ Leaves
- ☐ Crayons
- ☐ *The Creative Curriculum*, Appendix, p. 424

Preparation

Review pages 403–405 and the appendix, p. 424, "Goals and Objectives at a Glance," in *The Creative Curriculum*.

Survey the outdoor space near the workshop location to determine whether participants will be able to go outside and collect leaves. If you do not find a location or if participants will not be able to take a walk during the workshop, bring enough leaves for each table. Have artificial leaves, construction paper leaves, coloring book pictures of leaves, and a package of crayons for each table.

Introduction

Ask participants to think back to when they were children and played outdoors. Have them reflect on the following questions and discuss their experiences in small groups:

- What did you like to do outdoors?
- What materials did you enjoy playing with most?
- With whom did you play?
- What were adults doing as you played outdoors?

Bring the group together and ask what big ideas came from their discussions.

Make the following points:

- The outdoors offers an exciting environment for infants, toddlers, and twos when they can freely and safely explore.
- Making discoveries outdoors is exciting and invigorating for young children.
- Children can learn a lot from firsthand experiences outdoors.

Activity

Form groups of four or five people. Have each group chose one person to be the recorder and another person to be the timekeeper.

Give the following instructions:

- Take a 15-minute walk outdoors and talk about the discoveries children could make about leaves. The recorder should write down each discovery.

- During your walk, collect a variety of leaves to bring back to the room.

- The timekeeper will let you know when 15 minutes are up and it's time to return.

When participants return, ask them to continue exploring the leaves and sharing ideas of what children can learn about them. Be sure to advise participants to check the safety of a leaf (for example, is it poisonous?) before bringing it to their program.

Have each group report on one discovery children could make, and record each group's idea on chart paper. Continue hearing one idea at a time from each group until you have a complete list of the discoveries identified by participants.

Refer participants to the appendix, page 424, "Goals and Objectives at a Glance," in *The Creative Curriculum*. Have them identify which objectives could be addressed as children observe, collect, and play with leaves.

Next, give each table some of the artificial leaves to play with and examine. Ask participants to tell you what discoveries on the list children could *not* make if they had only artificial leaves to play with. Cross out each one as it is identified. Repeat this with the construction paper leaves and then with the coloring book picture and crayons. Note whether any of the discoveries children could make from experiences with natural leaves remain on the chart.

Summary

Make the following points:

- Going outdoors is important for children's health and well-being.

- The outdoors is a new environment to explore and learn about.

- Firsthand experiences offer rich opportunities for learning.

WORKSHOP

Keeping Children Safe and Healthy Outdoors

☐ Chart paper
☐ Markers
☐ Masking tape
☐ *The Creative Curriculum,* pp. 406–408

Preparation

Review pages 406–408 in *The Creative Curriculum.*

Introduction

Make the following points:

- A primary responsibility when taking children outdoors is to ensure their health and safety.

- Careful planning and close supervision will help you meet the challenges in taking very young children outdoors.

Activity

Provide each table with a piece of chart paper and markers and give the following instructions:

- Draw a line down the middle of your chart paper. At the top of the left side, write "Health and Safety Challenges." On the right-hand column, write "What Teachers Can Do."

- Spend a few minutes talking about potential dangers and health hazards you have encountered in taking infants, toddlers, and twos outdoors.

- When you have identified the challenges, identify what you might do to address the challenges and keep children safe and healthy outdoors.

Refer participants to pages 406–408 in *The Creative Curriculum* for additional strategies to keep children safe and healthy outdoors.

Have each group post its chart and invite participants to walk about and read each chart. Ask them to look for ideas that particularly interest them and that they will try in their program. Invite participants to share something they will use.

Summary

Make the following points:

- It's important to prepare an outdoor area that is appropriate and safe for very young children and then to supervise their use of the area.

- Daily monitoring of equipment and the outdoor area is essential to keeping children safe and healthy.

Designing Your Ideal Outdoor Area

☐ Chart paper
☐ Markers
☐ Masking tape
☐ *The Creative Curriculum*, pp. 409–420

Preparation

Review pages 409–420 in *The Creative Curriculum*.

If possible, take photos of outdoor areas used by children under age 3. Include play areas that are ideal as well as those that are not appealing.

Introduction

Make the following points:

- Because taking young children outdoors is so important to their health and well-being, it's important to spend time planning spaces that are appealing and appropriately challenging.

- The spaces and experiences you provide will vary, depending on the age of the children and what you have to work with in your outdoor space.

Activity

If you have made a collection of photos of outdoor play areas for children under age 3, show them or place them on tables so participants can review them. Ask:

- What features do you like?

- What are some things you want to avoid in your outdoor area?

Give each table group a set of markers and chart paper and the following instructions:

- You have just received a grant to build an ideal playground for your children.

- Decide if you want to design this playground for infants 6 weeks to 18 months of age or for toddlers and twos.

- Review pages 409–414 in *The Creative Curriculum*, focusing on the information relevant to your age-group.

- Talk about what you want in your playground and draw a picture of what it would look like. Think about what surfaces, equipment, and materials you want.

As the groups complete their drawings, refer participants to pages 415–420 in *The Creative Curriculum*. Have them identify tips for teachers on how to use their playground most effectively and what they can do to make outdoor experiences enjoyable for children.

Have the groups present their drawings and share the tips they would give other teachers.

Summary

Make the following points:

- The more appropriate and appealing the playground is for young children, the more enjoyable outdoor experiences will be for them.

- As always, your enjoyment of their experiences and your interactions with children as they play outdoors support their learning and development.